# Regulating Agricultural Markets in India

## Policy Studies Series

The Orient BlackSwan 'Policy Studies Series' is designed to fill a visible gap in existing Social Sciences literature: the need to address, empirically investigate and rigorously analyse public policy in the field of governance.

It is important to study the policy world in its entirety because:

- Policies establish the context within which we live out our individual and collective lives and deeply impact the way we and future generations will live and work.
- Policymaking and implementation is a process that is deeply embedded in politics, and serves as an entry point into the politics of a country.
- Public administrators, scholars, journalists, and specialists need to understand the relationship between knowledge systems, technology and the making of policy, the nature of public participation and responses, and how politicians seek to forge networks to ensure that policy is transformed into law.
- Policymaking highlights the linkages between domestic and global contexts. Ideas disseminated through global institutions and civil society networks impact policymaking insofar as they influence identification of problems and propose resolutions.

The literature generated through the series, we hope, will serve to identify the strength and lacunae of the making of policy and its implementation in India.

# Regulating Agricultural Markets in India

## A Smallholder Perspective

Sukhpal Singh

Orient BlackSwan

REGULATING AGRICULTURAL MARKETS IN INDIA:
A SMALLHOLDER PERSPECTIVE

**ORIENT BLACKSWAN PRIVATE LIMITED**

*Registered Office*
3-6-752 Himayatnagar, Hyderabad 500 029, Telangana, India
e-mail: centraloffice@orientblackswan.com

*Other Offices*
Bengaluru, Chennai, Guwahati, Hyderabad, Kolkata,
Mumbai, New Delhi, Noida, Patna


First published by Orient Blackswan Private Limited 2023

ISBN 978-93-5442-465-6

041673

*Typeset in*
ITC Berkeley Oldstyle Std 10.5/14
by Le Studio Graphique, Gurgaon 122 007

*Printed in India at*
Avantika Printers Private Limited, New Delhi 110 020

*Published by*
Orient Blackswan Private Limited
3-6-752 Himayatnagar, Hyderabad 500 029, Telangana, India
e-mail: info@orientblackswan.com

# Contents

# Abbreviations

| | |
|---|---|
| ACU | Adult Cattle Unit |
| APLCFSA | Agricultural Produce and Livestock Contract Farming and Services (Promotion and Facilitation) Act, 2018 |
| APLMA | Agricultural Produce and Livestock Marketing (Promotion and Facilitation) Act, 2017 |
| APMC | Agricultural Produce Market Committee |
| BKS | Bharatiya Kisan Sangh |
| BPL | Below Poverty Line |
| CA | Commission Agent |
| CACP | Commission for Agricultural Costs and Prices |
| CCFC | Chief Contract Farming Commissioner |
| CCI | Cotton Corporation of India |
| CFCs | Contract Farming Commissioners |
| CFSB | Contract Farming and Services Board |
| CUTS | Consumer Unity & Trust Society |
| CV | Coefficient of Variation |
| DBTs | Direct Benefit Transfers |
| DPP | Deficiency Price Payment |
| ECA | Essential Commodities (Amendment) Act |
| e-NAM | electronic-National Agriculture Market |
| F&V | Fruit and Vegetable |
| FAO | Food and Agriculture Organization (UN) |
| FCI | Food Corporation of India |

| | |
|---|---|
| FCMY | Farmer-Consumer Market Yard |
| FDI | Foreign Direct Investment |
| FHP | Farm Harvest Price |
| FPC | Farmer Producer Company |
| FPO | Farmer Producer Organisation |
| FPTC | Farmers' Produce Trade and Commerce (Promotion and Facilitation) Act, 2020 |
| FRP | Fair and Remunerative Price |
| GLOBALG.A.P. | Global Good Agricultural Practices (GAP) |
| GRMSP | Guaranteed Remunerative Minimum Support Price |
| GSAMB | Gujarat State Agricultural Marketing Board |
| GVP | Gross Value Product |
| ICRISAT | International Crops Research Institute for the Semi-Arid Tropics |
| ICT | Information and Communications Technology |
| IISD | International Institute for Sustainable Development |
| IPR | Intellectual Property Regime |
| KVK | Krishi Vikas Kendra |
| LSS | Lok Sabha Secretariat |
| MoAFW | Ministry of Agriculture and Farmer Welfare |
| MDF | Marketing Development Fund |
| MGNREGA | Mahatma Gandhi National Rural Employment Guarantee Act |
| MIS | Market Intervention Scheme |
| MNI | Market of National Importance |
| MPSAMB | Madhya Pradesh State Agricultural Marketing Board |
| MRP | Minimum Reserved Price |
| MSP | Minimum Support Price |
| NAFED | National Agricultural Cooperative Marketing Federation of India |

| | |
|---|---|
| NCT | National Capital Territory |
| NGO | Non-Governmental Organisation |
| NSA | Net Sown Area |
| NSO | National Statistical Office |
| PACS | Primary Agricultural Credit Societies |
| PC | Producer Company |
| PCMY | Producer-Consumer Market Yard |
| PDS | Public Distribution System |
| PMO | Primary Marketing Organisation |
| PMY | Primary Market Yard |
| PPP | Public-Private Partnership |
| RKM | Rashtriya Kisan Manch |
| SAMB | State Agricultural Marketing Board |
| SAP | State Advised Price |
| SC | Scheduled Caste |
| SCM | Special Commodity Markets |
| SFAC | Small Farmers' Agri-Business Consortium |
| SHG | Self-Help Groups |
| SKM | Samyukta Kisan Morcha |
| SMY | Sub-Market Yards |
| SP | Superintendent of Police |
| ST | Scheduled Tribe |
| UMP | Unified Market Platform |
| UPA | United Progressive Alliance |
| USAID | United States Agency for International Development |
| UT | Union Territory |
| VMSS | Vyapar Mandal Sahyog Samiti |

# Figures and Tables

## Figures



## Tables

# Preface

Small producers have dominated agriculture and allied sectors for a long time now and they contribute significantly to farm output and employment. But they suffer from many market disadvantages due to the small size of their holdings despite being more efficient producers, as the market does not work for them most of the time in most states of India. The Union government has been attempting to reform agricultural markets in various ways for some time now though constitutionally, this falls under the state domain of policy and law making. Initially, the Union government had been proposing the model for such reforms by way of proposing to states the Model APMC Acts and more recently, even the Model Contract Farming Act (2018). But it was only in 2020 during the Covid-19 pandemic, that the Union government undertook the route of ordinances first, and the subsequent enactment of agricultural market laws at its own level, overlooking the fact that most of the states had by then amended their APMC Acts and had provided for most of the provisions as contained in the Model APMC Acts since 2003. It was this step which led to the now historic farmer protests and agitation over more than a year on the borders of Delhi and finally, repeal of the two new and one amended Farm Acts by the Union government in late 2021. The farm unions saw these Union Acts, popularly known as the Farm Bills, as a direct attack on their livelihoods, wherein they found these enactments meant state withdrawal from agricultural markets and saw decline of public agricultural markets (APMCs) as the immediate risk, and privatisation of agricultural trade and even land market as the long-term risk. I wrote and spoke on the new Acts across various fora during the course of the agitation and the various rounds of negotiations among the government and the farmer unions, and even immediately after the Acts were repealed.

The present study critically examines various Model Acts and the two new Acts of 2020 (repealed in 2021) and their contents from a smallholder perspective, and even addresses the legality of the farmer unions' demand for legalising MSP for all crops for which it is declared. Finally, it sums up the issues with various types of agricultural market reforms, and infers possible measures to improve the performance of agricultural markets for smallholder farmers, who are generally excluded from MSP delivery mechanisms for various reasons. The book focuses only on regulatory aspects of the reforms and does not address policy aspects by design.

I thank Dr A. R. Vasavi for encouraging me to put together all my analyses of agricultural markets, especially of the new Farm Acts of 2020 in one place in the form of this book, including updating some of the analysis in the light of recent developments, and for introducing me to Orient BlackSwan (OBS), which led to this journey of producing this book. At OBS, I am thankful to Roopa Sharma for getting the proposal approved and commissioning the manuscript, and to Debangana Pal for editing of the manuscript in an extremely professional and competent manner in a short period of time and making sure that all permissions and acknowledgements are in place. I also acknowledge with thanks the contributions of Nilanjana Majumdar for overseeing the publication schedule of the book, Suchetana Ghosh Dostidar for in-house proofreading support, and other supporting staff at OBS for their contribution in various ways to the timely publication of this book. I am thankful to various publications and institutions—the *Economic and Political Weekly, Social Change*, The Hindu Centre of Politics and Public Policy, and Institute of Development Studies, Jaipur for permitting me to use some of my own work on the topics of agricultural markets and market channels, which had been published by them earlier, during and immediately after the farmer agitation on Farm Acts.

I hope that the book will interest agricultural market researchers, development experts, policy makers, students of agricultural markets, farmer interest groups, non-governmental organisations, and other agencies and stakeholders in the farm sector, and help them understand the dynamics of agricultural markets from the smallholder livelihood perspective.

SUKHPAL SINGH
Ahmedabad, September 2023

# Publishers' Acknowledgements

The publishers would like to thank the following publications, institutions, and individuals for granting kind permission to use in the present volume some material previously published by them.

Chapter 1 or the 'Introduction' of the present volume draws heavily from the Prof. V. S. Vyas Memorial Lecture delivered by the author at the Institute of Development Studies (IDS), Jaipur on 21 October 2021. This was later published by the IDS as Singh, Sukhpal. 2022. 'Contextualising the Repealed 2020 Union Agricultural Markets Acts in Farmer Income (Policy) Debate', Prof. V. S. Vyas Memorial Lecture, IDS Jaipur, July, and has been reproduced with revisions here with their kind permission.

Table 1.7 titled 'State and Scheme-wise Farmer Income Support Programmes in India' has been reproduced with kind permission of Kavitha H. N. The table was first published in Kavitha, H. N., Pramod Kumar, P. Anbukkani, R. Burman, and P. Prakash. 2021. 'Income Support Schemes Evaluation of PM KISAN vis-à-vis State Government Schemes'. *Economic and Political Weekly* 56(34): 13–17.

Chapter 2 of the present volume has a section called 'Major Conceptual, Policy and Governance Issues in Model APLMA, 2017'. This section was published earlier in 2018 as part of an article by the author in the *Economic and Political Weekly* titled

'Reforming Agricultural Markets in India: A Tale of Two Model Acts', and has been reproduced here with permission.

Chapter 3 of the present volume titled 'Legislating Contract Farming Practice: The Model Contract Farming Act, 2018' was first published as part of an article by the author in the *Economic and Political Weekly* titled 'Reforming Agricultural Markets in India: A Tale of Two Model Acts', and has been reproduced here with permission.

Chapter 3 Appendix Figures 3.1 3.3 and 3.5 have been reproduced with permission from *Economic and Political Weekly*, where they had been first published in the 2004 article by the author titled, 'Crisis and Diversification in Punjab Agriculture: Role of State and Agribusiness'. *Economic and Political Weekly* 39(52): 5583–5590.

Chapter 3 Appendix Figures 3.2, 3.4, 3.6, and 3.7 have been reproduced with permission of Prof. Riaz Ahmad, Editor, *Social Change,* Centre for Social Development, New Delhi. The figures had been originally published in Singh, Sukhpal. 2005. 'Changing Structure and Organisation of Agriculture and Small Farmers in India'. *Social Change* 35: 1–31.

A part of Chapter 4 of this volume titled 'The Farmers' Produce Trade and Commerce (Promotion and Facilitation) Act, 2020: Inadequate Rationale and Implications' was first published as an online article by The Hindu Centre for Politics and Public Policy in March 2021 as Singh, Sukhpal. 2021. 'Food Security and Markets: Understanding the Protests over India's Changing Social Contract with Farmers', *The Hindu Centre for Politics and Public Policy*, 15 March. Available at https://www.thehinducentre.com/the-arena/current-issues/article34060554.ece (accessed August 2023). It has been reproduced here in a revised form with their kind permission.

An earlier version of Chapter 5 in this volume titled 'The Union Contract Farming Act, 2020: Issues and Implications' was first published online by The Hindu Centre for Politics and Public Policy as part of an article: Singh, Sukhpal. 2021. 'Food Security and Markets: Understanding the Protests over India's Changing Social Contract with Farmers', *The Hindu Centre for Politics and Public Policy*, 15 March. Available at https://www.thehinducentre.com/the-arena/current-issues/article34060554.ece (accessed August 2023). A more updated version of The Hindu Centre article was later published as an article in the *Economic and Political Weekly*: Singh, Sukhpal. 2022. 'The (Repealed) Union Contract Farming Act, 2020: Corporatising Indian Agriculture'. *Economic and Political Weekly* 57(2). Available at https://www.epw.in/journal/2022/2/commentary/repealed-union-contract-farming-act-2020.html (accessed August 2023). The present chapter has been reproduced here in a revised form with the kind permission of The Hindu Centre for Politics and Public Policy and the *Economic and Political Weekly*.

one

# Introduction*

## Background and Context

The Indian agricultural market Acts of 2020, popularly known as the Farm Laws, which were a set of three legislations—two new laws and an amendment to the existing Essential Commodities Act (ECA)—resulted in a series of protests by farmers outside the national capital. These three laws aimed to create a 'One Nation, One Market' framework in India which is essentially a federal nation, albeit with a unitary bias. The two new Union laws passed were the Farmers' Produce Trade and Commerce (Promotion and Facilitation) Act, 2020, and the Farmers (Empowerment and Protection) Agreement on Price Assurance and Farm Services Act, 2020, also known as the Contract Farming Act, 2020. The third legislative measure was an amendment, to remove uncertainties regarding stocking limits on food commodities, which were provided for under the ECA to contain price volatility, a not-too-uncommon feature in commodity markets. Also, the two new Union Acts were on agricultural markets which, according to the

*This chapter draws heavily from the Prof. V. S. Vyas Memorial Lecture delivered by the author at the Institute of Development Studies (IDS), Jaipur on 21 October 2021. This was later published by the IDS as Singh (2022), and has been reproduced here with their kind permission.

sharing of legislative powers in the Indian Constitution, are under the domain of state governments.

The three contentious Farm Laws mentioned above were repealed in 2021 (*The Indian Express* 2021) after a year-long resistance from farmer groups. These Acts need to be understood in the context of Indian agriculture and smallholder livelihoods, as they represent a fundamental reorientation of the existing regulatory framework of Indian agriculture into a package of 'reform' measures, which open up the domains of production, trade, and storage to the private sector like never before, and some of them like the Contract Farming Act bring the mandi to the farm, in terms of buyers not only going to the farm to buy farm produce but also influencing what (crop, variety and quality) and how it will be produced (package of practices) in the farm.[1]

The (un)stated objectives of the new laws include: One Nation, One Market (i.e., going beyond e-NAM which was at the individual APMC level only);[2] freedom of channel choice for farmers; barrier-free inter-state trade, which is already a Union List subject but it is argued that inter-state trade can bring about an 11 per cent increase in farm prices; barrier-free intra-state trade; and a framework for e-trading of farm produce with the overall objective of attracting private investment in agricultural markets. The stated purpose behind these laws was to provide better price discovery for the farmer and to make agricultural markets attractive for private investment.

In effect, the three Acts aimed to provide 'Ease of Doing Business' for India's corporate sector right from procurement to stocking, processing, and retailing as value chain players. Therein lie the apprehensions of the protesting farmers who spent more than one year camping at the Haryana and Uttar Pradesh borders outside Delhi. In addition to the protesting farmers, the Acts have attracted serious opposition from as many as six states—Punjab, Chhattisgarh, Delhi, Rajasthan, Kerala, and West Bengal—which have passed resolutions against these new Acts (Singh 2021), from various farmers' unions, many civil society organisations, and a large number of political parties, despite the Union government claiming and highlighting various benefits of the new Acts at several fora and in Parliament. Moreover, three State governments—Punjab, Chhattisgarh, and Rajasthan—even tried to amend the Union Acts at their level but the respective governors have not given their assent (ibid.).

That is why the Acts invited such large-scale and entrenched farmer protest for more than a year at the borders of Delhi that led to the government withdrawing these Acts altogether in November 2021. Before that, the Supreme Court of India had stayed the implementation of these Acts in January 2021 and set up a committee of experts to listen to the grievances of the farmers relating to these Farm Laws and the views of the government and to make recommendations (SC Committee 2021). It is a different matter that the farmers' unions did not recognise the Supreme Court-appointed committee due to its very composition and it became infructuous as the Farm Laws were repealed altogether by the government before the report became unofficially public in March 2022. The Committee itself went overboard and instead of talking to the protesting farmers and the government, recommended reforms which go beyond the contested Farm Acts; for example, it recommended that the suspension of Farm Laws would be unfair to the silent majority of the farmers who supported them (ibid.). It also made many other far-reaching recommendations which will be discussed in the following chapters of this volume as appropriate.

Among the many demands of the farmer unions, the most prominent were the repeal of the three Farm Laws and making Minimum Support Price (MSP) a legal right for farmers, though the latter is still unresolved. Since the farmers' protest was unprecedented in terms of its scale as well as endurance for a long period of time, it brought back focus on agricultural market reforms, which were posited as corporatisation of the farm sector, and it was argued that such reforms will only perpetuate the farm crisis in India. It is also important to underline that the agrarian crisis has been a live issue for some time in India now, as reflected in the spate of farmer suicides over the last two decades and the rising indebtedness of the Indian farmer as seen from official data from various sources. And this crisis has been discussed in the context of small-farm-dominated nature of the agrarian economy.

More recently, questions are being asked about the relevance of smallholders for achieving higher agricultural growth and raising food production to meet its growing demand (Murphy 2011). The term 'smallholder' is a relative one in that it refers to limited resource endowments of such farmers *relative* to those of other farmers in the sector in each local context. Thus, the definition of small can differ across countries, and agro-ecological zones within countries, such as, irrigated plains and hill areas where one hectare can be small versus drylands or rainfed regions where even 10-hectare farms may be considered small (Vermeulen and Cotula 2010). Though globally, farming is dominated by smallholders with 500 million of them supporting two billion people (Vorley et al. 2012), yet the global polices and processes of change indicate a large-farm focus (Dev 2012), and agricultural policies and programmes are biased against smallholders. Also, the emerging investment climate supports only a small fraction of the smallholders (2–10 per cent) who are resourceful or have access to assets and can be attractive to large private buyers (Vorley et al. 2012). Also, generally, 'one size fits all' polices are recommended and implemented which does not help small farmers, and rather puts them at a disadvantage against other categories. A recent study (Foster and Rosenzweig 2022) based on Indian village and household data of ICRISAT (International Crops Research Institute for the Semi-Arid Tropics) across 18 villages in five states and covering the period of 2009–14 with a panel survey of 819 farmers claims that for an Indian farm to be efficient and for maximum labour productivity to be reaped, the optimal size of the land should be 24 acres (against 2.71 acres at present), which will mean that the number of farms in India will go down by 82 per cent from the present and income per farm worker will increase by 68 per cent! This is based on the assumption that a sprayer is an indicator of technology and mechanisation in agriculture which if used on a scale (larger farms) can replace labour and enhance the productivity of remaining labour (farmers and farm workers) and give this kind of efficiency.

But the role of small farmers in poverty reduction is well recognised and there is evidence to that effect in terms of agricultural growth being twice as effective as growth outside agriculture (Dev 2012; Vorley et al. 2012). India being smallholder-dominated (85 per cent of all operated holdings being marginal or small, that is, less than two ha., with 63 per cent holdings being smaller than one ha. each), her agricultural economy cannot be discussed without bringing into focus the issues of such small operators of land. Given that the average size of holding in India is decreasing over the years, it is even more compelling to examine smallholder issues and concerns in the increasingly globalised agricultural market context. Small farms are more irrigated than their larger counterparts though more from groundwater and many times with water bought from other farmers under some arrangement. They also contribute 19 per cent (in Punjab) to 86 per cent (in West Bengal) of farm output across the Indian states but overall contribute 51 per cent of output with 46 per cent of operated land share in India, and a much higher share

(70 per cent) in high-value crops like vegetables and milk. But small farmers are less literate and are more from marginalised castes and communities like Scheduled Castes and Scheduled Tribes and generally excluded from modern market arrangements like contract farming or direct purchase (Dev 2012; Singh 2012a, 2012b). Recent studies (Chand et al. 2011; Gaurav and Mishra 2011) show that small farms produce as much as or higher value of output on an average per unit area than that by medium or large farms which refutes the argument that small farms cannot be the future of Indian agriculture.

Also, it is important to recognise that the viability of the small farm versus the small farmer are two different issues. Small farms may produce more output per unit relatively but that income may not be adequate in many situations for farmer family sustenance (Chand et al. 2011). This is the context for the argument for non-farm sources of income for small farmer families. But it is clear that if a majority of Indian smallholders are going to remain dependent on farming for some time to come, then it is crucial that ways and mechanisms of making small farms deliver livelihoods are debated and discussed, and role of policy assessed so that appropriate policy and practical ways could be discerned.

However, small farmers are not a homogenous group. There are small farmers who are fully commercialised and buy and sell in markets. There are others who participate in the market in a limited manner to buy inputs and sell some part of their output. There are still others who are subsistence farmers consuming most of their farm production while selling labour in the market or buying foodgrains from the market to meet their total consumption needs, thus becoming net buyers of food. Within commercial agriculture, from a markets perspective, there are again specific segments of farming community including small farmers: First, there are small farmers who are into high-value export markets either directly, or through Primary Marketing Organisations (PMOs), like in grapes and baby corn, or indirectly through exporters like in gherkins. Second, there are small farmers who are fully commercialised and operate in domestic high-value markets, for example, in vegetables like potato, onion, and other vegetables, who supply to wholesale markets or modern domestic retail or wholesale 'cash and carry' players. Third, there are small farmers who are into cereals and oilseed or pulses and sell in domestic open markets locally or in Agricultural Produce Market Committee (APMC) or regulated markets. Finally, there are small farmers in Green Revolution regions and even elsewhere who produce for the state and depend on the Minimum Support Price (MSP) policy, for wheat, paddy, cotton, and some oilseeds. Further, there is an emerging segment of organic producers who are either into export markets directly or through private agencies, or non-governmental organisations (NGOs), or cater to domestic fresh and processed food markets. Further, there are small or family or peasant farmers, corporate farmers, and entrepreneurial farmers, with each group differing in their approach to farming and interface with markets. The peasant mode practised by small or family farmers is: co-production and co-evolution, distantation from input markets, output side differentiation, craft and skill-oriented technologies, labour (quantity and quality)-based intensification, multi-functional, reciprocal relations between farms, continuity from past to future, high level of value added and increasing social wealth. On the other hand, entrepreneurial mode is: disconnected from nature, artificial mode of farming, high market dependence, high level of commoditisation, entrepreneur and mechanical tech-centred, high per centage of rented land, scale-dominant trajectory, technology-led intensification and specialised competitive relations and break of past and future, low level of value added, and contains and redistributes social wealth. Entrepreneurial agriculture is the outcome of the Green Revolution and rural development programmes (der Ploeg 2018), and agri outsourcing as the emerging mode of farming has led to a situation where the only tool of an entrepreneur farmer is: telephone/mobile. Besides small farmers, other rural poor whose fortunes are linked to agriculture and its markets directly or indirectly are: landless agricultural labour, pastoralists, and artisans.

Increasingly, smallholder agriculture is back on the policy agenda globally due to its relevance in meeting the growing demand for food, and improving and sustaining rural livelihoods in developing countries. Small-farms (defined as being < 2 ha.) accounted for 84 per cent of all farms globally and operated only 12 per cent of the global available farmland. The smallest two farm size classes (0–1 ha. and 1–2 ha.) were the greatest contributors to global food production compared to all other classes, producing 28–31 per cent of total crop production and 30–34 per cent of the global food supply with 24 per cent of harvested area operated by them. Smallholders (again, farms < 2 ha.) also allocated the largest percentage (55–59 per cent) of their crop production to food compared to all other farm size classes (Ricciardia et al. 2018). Similarly, in China, these small farms are 98 per cent of the total number of farms and in Ethiopia small farms constitute 87 per cent of all farms with 60 per cent of the total cultivated area. Small farms, including marginal and almost landless holdings, account for 90 per cent of owned holdings with 43 per cent of total owned area and 89 per cent of all operational holdings with 54 per cent of the total cultivated area in India (Tables 1.1 and 1.2). This gap between owned and operated holdings is accounted for by leasing in and leasing out with 17 per cent of holdings being leased, accounting for 13 per cent of operated area in 2018–19 (Table 1.3).

**Table 1.1: Percentage distribution of number of holdings and area owned by size category of ownership holdings during 2018–19, 2012–13, and 2002–03**

| *Size category of household ownership holdings (in ha.)* | *Percentage distribution of landholdings* | | | *Percentage distribution of area owned* | | |
|---|---|---|---|---|---|---|
| | *2018–19* | *2012–13* | *2002–03* | *2018–19* | *2012–13* | *2002–03* |
| Landless (≤ 0.002) | 8.2 | 7.4 | 10.0 | 0.0 | 0.0 | 0.0 |
| Marginal (0.002–1.000) | 76.5 | 75.4 | 69.6 | 34.5 | 29.8 | 23.0 |
| Small (1.0–2.0) | 9.3 | 10.0 | 10.8 | 24.9 | 23.5 | 20.4 |
| Semi-medium (2.0–4.0) | 4.4 | 5.0 | 6.0 | 22.0 | 22.1 | 22.0 |
| Medium (4.0–10.0) | 1.4 | 1.9 | 3.0 | 14.7 | 18.8 | 23.1 |
| Large (>10.0) | 0.1 | 0.2 | 0.5 | 3.9 | 5.8 | 11.6 |
| **All sizes** | **100.0** | **100.0** | **100.0** | **100.0** | **100.0** | **100.0** |

*Note*: Figures may not add up to 100 since they have been rounded off.

*Source*: NSO (2021).

**Table 1.2: Percentage distribution of number of operational holdings and percentage distribution of area operated by size category of operational holdings in 2018–19 versus 2012–13 and 2002–03**

| *Size category of operational holdings (in ha.)* | *Percentage distribution of number of operational holdings* | | | | *Percentage distribution of area operated* | | | |
|---|---|---|---|---|---|---|---|---|
| | *2018–19* | *2012–13* | *2002–03* | | *2018–19* | *2012–13* | *2002–03* | |
| | | | *Kharif* | *Rabi* | | | *Kharif* | *Rabi* |
| Landless (≤0.002) | 0.0 | 0.0 | – | – | | | – | – |
| Marginal (0.002–1.0) | 72.6 | 73.2 | 69.8 | 70.0 | 31.7 | 27.7 | 22.6 | 21.7 |
| Small (1.0–2.0) | 16.4 | 15.3 | 16.2 | 15.9 | 24.7 | 23.4 | 20.9 | 20.3 |
| Semi-medium (2.0–4.0) | 8.0 | 8.1 | 9.0 | 8.9 | 22.0 | 23.5 | 22.5 | 22.3 |
| Medium (4.0–10.0) | 2.7 | 3.0 | 4.2 | 4.4 | 16.2 | 19.3 | 22.2 | 23.1 |
| Large (>10.0) | 0.3 | 0.4 | 0.8 | 0.8 | 5.4 | 6.0 | 11.8 | 12.5 |
| **All sizes** | **100.0** | **100.0** | **100.0** | **100.0** | **100.0** | **100.0** | **100.0** | **100.0** |

*Note*: Figures may not add up to 100 due to rounding.

*Source*: NSO (2021).

**Table 1.3: Percentage of tenant holdings and area leased-in during 2018–19, 2012–13, and 2002–03**

| *Year* | *Percentage of tenant holdings* | *Percentage of area leased-in* |
|---|---|---|
| 2018–2019 | 17.3 | 13.0 |
| 2012–2013 | 13.7 | 11.3 |
| 2002–2003 | 9.9 | 6.5 |

*Note*: 'Tenant holding' stands for an operational holding with wholly or partially leased-in area.

*Source*: NSO (2021).

The NSO survey found that in 2018–19, 34 per cent of the households were submarginal and 36 per cent marginal besides 17.7 per cent being small. The average area owned per household declined from 0.7 ha. per household to 0.6 ha. in 2013 and 0.5 ha. in 2019. Forty-five per cent to 50 per cent of the leased-out land was for fixed money and 25 per cent on share of produce. In terms of operational landholding distribution, small category accounted for 16.4 per cent of the total holdings with 24.7 per cent of area operated compared with 15 per cent and 23 per cent of landholdings and operated area, respectively, in 2012–13. Altogether in 2018–19, marginal and small categories accounted for 89 per cent of the operational holdings and 56 per cent of the operated area. The percentage of tenant holdings as well as area leased increased from less than 14 per cent and 11 per cent respectively in 2012–13 to 17.3 per cent and 13 per cent in 2018–19 (NSO 2021).

Further, dryland agriculture supports 40 per cent of the human population and 60 per cent of the livestock population in India. It produces 44 per cent of food requirements, and thus it has and will continue to play a critical role in India's food security. However, aberrant behaviour of monsoon rainfall results in frequent droughts that impact resource-poor farmers. Drylands account for 53 per cent of total cropped area, with 48 per cent of the area under food crops and 68 per cent under non-food crops. In terms of production, drylands account for nearly 80 per cent of the output of coarse cereals, 50 per cent of maize, 65 per cent of chickpea and pigeonpea, 81 per cent of groundnut, and 88 per cent of soyabean. Half the output of cotton in India is from the dry districts (Shankar 2006). Dry regions are economically fragile regions which are highly vulnerable to environmental stress and shocks. Degraded soils with low water-holding capacities along with multiple nutrient deficiencies and depleting groundwater table contributes to low crop yields, further leading to land degradation (Vijayan 2016). Nine states (Rajasthan, Madhya Pradesh, Maharashtra, Gujarat, Chhattisgarh, Jharkhand, Andhra Pradesh, Karnataka, and Tamil Nadu) account for over 80 per cent of the drylands. Annual rainfall in the drylands varies from less than 150 mm to 1600 mm. Traditional cropping systems use diverse strategies like mixed-cropping and intercropping for rainfall insurance. The crop combinations and sequences are often highly complex and have come up taking into consideration minute variations in soil type, depth, crop maturity and susceptibility to rainfall fluctuations, and household needs. As many as 60 crop mixes are reported to have existed in villages of peninsular India (Shankar 2006).

Forty per cent of India's Net Sown Area (NSA) is in 323 rainfed districts and 54 per cent in irrigated districts. Agro-climatologically, the soil erosion (by wind, water) is the highest in arid rainfed districts (57 per cent) while it is the lowest in irrigated arid districts (17 per cent). It was the highest in Rajasthan (60 per cent) and the lowest in Punjab and Haryana (7 per cent each). Small and marginal farmers in rainfed districts accounted for 73 per cent of all farmers. The area owned by them was 43 per cent in rainfed districts and 51 per cent in irrigated districts (Venkateswarlu 2017). They suffer high product and market risks.

Many of the poorest districts of India fall in rainfed areas and these regions support a significant proportion of Indian livestock and contribute significantly to Indian agriculture. Livestock ($ACU/km^2$) density over 600 districts was $112/km^2$. It was $88/km^2$ in 313 rainfed districts and $145/km^2$ in 287 irrigated districts. Evidently, small ruminants dominate in rainfed districts and are very important for local livelihoods. In contrast to goats, the density of sheep is much higher in rainfed areas. Sheep are largely part of the grazing economy. They are inexpensive to maintain and provide wool, meat, and manure. The 100 poorest districts that are rainfed belong to the states of Arunachal Pradesh, Assam, Bihar, Chhattisgarh, Jharkhand, Madhya Pradesh, Nagaland, Meghalaya, Odisha, and West Bengal. Harriss-White called these areas

> "...India's rainfed agricultural dystopia," characterised by an increasingly risk-beset, polarized and indebted agrarian capitalism dominated by micro-production and its credit and exchange relations. The mass of small-scale farms are not "un-incorporated", they are incorporated in a differentiated way such that much agriculture is a part-time component of a complex livelihood portfolio dominated by labouring (2008: 553).

Given its large size and extremely low yield levels, a rise in such yields and returns in this sector is likely to have the largest impact on livelihoods. Drylands are poor in terms of their banking networks. Informal credit markets with interest rates ranging from 60 to 120 per cent dominate. Due to low marketed surplus, many dryland areas have poorly developed commodity markets. Distress sale is common, often to the same trader who is also the lender. Creation of marketing networks through checking distress sales and pooling of whatever surplus the area produces, could be an income-generating activity (Shankar 2006).

There is no doubt that small farms maximise labour use and value added, and have higher yields, both of which are socially optimal, given land scarcity and labour surplus in developing countries. They also promote equity. It was due to small farms that rapid agricultural growth occurred in Korea, China, Japan, and Taiwan, and even parts of India. But employment which is the only way to raise farmers' incomes, is low on small farms because of the low employment elasticity of output due to nature of crops grown and technology used. Further, small farmers suffer from many market and institutional problems which lead to lower price realisation for their output besides higher transaction costs, though they are as much as or more productive than larger farms per unit area, for example, in India (Chand et al. 2011; Gaurav and Mishra 2011). But these studies also find that even with this higher productivity, the livelihoods of such smallholders are not viable as their expenses far exceed the net income from a small farm.

As Jan Douwe van der Ploeg argues:

> The strength of a farm does not reside only, or even primarily, in its size. It depends on how farming is organised and developed over time and how it interacts with the context in which it operates. Small farms can render a good income and enough savings to be reproduced over time, but they can also struggle and fail. The same is true of large farms (2018: 63).

He continues: 'Thus, the policy focus on large farms and the preferential allocation of development opportunities to them is, indeed, nothing but betting on a lame horse. Policies that would encourage small farms to grow would contribute far more to growth and development' (ibid.: 86). The evidence from China where the average size of farm is 0.5 ha and which yields twice of India's average shows that farm size does not matter. China's higher farm productivity is the result of a focus on high-value crops, mechanisation and animal-based products, besides afforestation. As a result, 59 per cent of China's GVP (Gross Value Product) was retained at the farmer level unlike only 23 per cent in the Netherlands. Therefore, what you do, how much, when, how, for whom and why, on a farm makes it viable or not.

## Farmer Income

The NSO Survey for 2018–19 covering 57,000 plus households estimated the number of agricultural households (defined as those earning at least Rs 4,000 per annum from farming and having at least one member self-employed in agriculture either in the principal status or in subsidiary status during the last 365 days) to be 93 million (54 per cent of all rural households). Seventy per cent of such households had less than one ha. land in their possession and only 0.4 per cent had more than 10 ha. each. Further, 69 per cent of these households were engaged in crop production and 2.3 per cent in livestock farming. Also, 14.2 per cent reported casual labour as the major source of employment and 7.7 per cent were regularly employed or salaried. The average area owned per household was 0.87 ha. and 2.6 per cent of the households were landless compared with 8.2 per cent of the rural households being landless. 3.2 per cent households reported leasing out land and 13.9 per cent reported leasing in, and the average area leased out and leased in for a household was 0.69 hectare and 0.48 hectare respectively. In total, 6.4 million households reported leasing out land and 22.8 million leasing in. The number of operated agricultural holdings was estimated to be 89.6 million and average area per operated holding was 1 ha., while average area operated per holding was 0.92 ha. If the non-agricultural households holding land were also included, then the estimated number of operational holdings turned out to be 102 million and operated average area per holding 0.9 ha. and average area operated for such holding 0.83 ha. Among the operational holdings, 72.6 per cent were marginal and 0.3 per cent large. Moreover, 17.3 per cent holdings were operated by tenants accounting for 13 per cent of the total area. The share of marginal category in total operated land was 31.7 per cent and that of the large category 5.4 per cent. Eighty-four per cent of the land was used for crop production and 6 per cent for both crop and animal husbandry while 0.6 per cent only for animal husbandry. The average number of cattle owned was 2.2 per household and 1.5 milk-yielding buffaloes per household, and 10.7 per cent households owned poultry birds averaging 1.3 per household. The SC households constituted 16 per cent of the total number of agricultural households and STs constituted 14.2 per cent. Whereas 92.7 per cent of agricultural households engaged in crop production in Kharif only, 72.5 per cent did so during Rabi season. The average value of crop production per household was Rs 46,277 in Kharif and Rs 5,807 during Rabi (NSO 2021).

The average monthly income per agricultural household was of the order of Rs 10,218 of which crop production accounted for 37.2 per cent, farming of animals another 15.5 per cent, making for a total of 52.7 per cent with the rest mostly coming from wages (39.8 per cent), non-farm business (6.3 per cent), and leasing out of agricultural land (1.3 per cent) (Table 1.4). The net income was even lower at Rs 3,058 per month (36.7 per cent of total) from crop farming and only Rs 441 (5 per cent of total) from animal farming (Table 1.5). The other dimension of the definition of an agricultural household in this round of Survey was that at least one member should be self-employed in agriculture as principal or subsidiary worker during the last year. This was the definition in terms of income cut-off for the receipts from the self-employed

**Table 1.4: Land class size wise average monthly income (Rs) per agricultural household from different sources during July 2018–June 2019 (ha.)**

| *Size class of land possessed (ha.)* | *Income from wages (Rs)* | *Income from leasing out of land (Rs)* | *Net receipt from crop production* (Rs)* | *Net receipt from farming of animals* (Rs)* | *Net receipt from non-farm business (Rs)* | *Total Income (Rs)* |
|---|---|---|---|---|---|---|
| <0.01 | 6,435 | 254 | 1,660 | 2,084 | 772 | 11,204 |
| 0.01–0.40 | 4,491 | 189 | 977 | 1,162 | 703 | 7,522 |
| 0.40–1.00 | 3,906 | 76 | 2,683 | 1,335 | 570 | 8,571 |
| 1.01–2.00 | 3,647 | 74 | 5,269 | 1,845 | 613 | 11,449 |
| 2.01–4.00 | 3,548 | 146 | 9,432 | 2,551 | 758 | 16,435 |
| 4.01–10.00 | 4,273 | 451 | 19,645 | 3,451 | 472 | 28,292 |
| 10.00+ | 3,943 | 581 | 43,599 | 11,473 | 1,162 | 60,758 |
| **All sizes** | **4,063** | **134** | **3,798** | **1,582** | **641** | **10,218** |

*Note*: *Only out-of-pocket expenses considered for working out net receipt.

*Source*: NSO (2021).

**Table 1.5: Average monthly income (Rs) per agricultural household from different sources during July 2018–June 2019 for each size class of land possessed (ha.)**

| *Size class of land possessed (ha.)* | *Income from wages (Rs)* | *Income from leasing out of land (Rs)* | *Net receipt from crop production* (Rs)* | *Net receipt from farming of animals* (Rs)* | *Net receipt from non-farm business (Rs)* | *Total Income (Rs)* |
|---|---|---|---|---|---|---|
| <0.01 | 6,435 | 254 | 1,435 | 1,087 | 772 | 9,982 |
| 0.01–0.40 | 4,491 | 189 | 657 | 349 | 703 | 6,388 |
| 0.40–1.00 | 3,906 | 76 | 2,042 | 356 | 570 | 6,951 |
| 1.01–2.00 | 3,647 | 74 | 4,313 | 541 | 613 | 9,189 |
| 2.01–4.00 | 3,548 | 146 | 7,945 | 600 | 758 | 12,997 |
| 4.01–10.00 | 4,273 | 451 | 16,914 | 342 | 472 | 22,453 |
| 10.00+ | 3,943 | 581 | 37,639 | 7,087 | 1,162 | 50,412 |
| **All sizes** | **4,063** | **134** | **3,058** | **441** | **641** | **8,337** |

*Note*: *Both the paid-out expenses and imputed expenses considered for working out net receipt.

*Source*: NSO (2021).

in agriculture during the last (17th) Survey round also. Even a household growing vegetables in a kitchen garden or flowers in the courtyard was considered as possessing an operational holding.

Major crops grown by the farmers in terms of agricultural households reporting them were paddy (53.2 per cent), maize (11.3 per cent), cotton (7.2 per cent), bajra (8.3 per cent), and soyabean (6 per cent) during Kharif and wheat (41.2 per cent), rapeseed/mustard (7.5 per cent), paddy (9.3 per cent), gram (6.7 per cent), and potato (5.3 per cent) during Rabi season. It is interesting to note that whereas 95 per cent households reported selling soyabean, cotton, and sugarcane during Kharif, and cotton and sugarcane (91 per cent and 96 per cent) during Rabi, paddy and wheat were sold by 53 per cent and 77 per cent in the two seasons and wheat by 51 per cent during the Rabi season. Mostly across crops, farmers sold in the local market followed by APMC market accounting for a high of 20 per cent of households in the case of soyabean and 25 per cent in case of arhar and 14 per cent in case of cotton. The cooperatives accounted for 21 per cent only in case of sugarcane in one season and 14 per cent in another season with the only other crop reaching 5 per cent being paddy. The government agencies fared even poorly with only 10–15 per cent households reporting selling to them sugarcane and 7 per cent paddy in Kharif and 13 per cent paddy in Rabi.

Surprisingly, the Farmer Producer Organisations (FPOs) were missing as sales channel with only 0.1 per cent households reporting them in paddy, cotton, and gram. The private processor has a significant interface with the farmers with 38 per cent selling sugarcane to such players in one season and 30 per cent in another season. Other major crops having such interface are cotton (6–9 per cent), groundnut (7 per cent), masoor (6 per cent), and paddy (4–6 per cent). Another major channel, that of contract farming, was also missing in most crops with the exception of sugarcane (3–6 per cent) and paddy (only 0.5 per cent of the households reported it). Further, in terms of the shares of different channels in the sold quantity, it was again local markets which followed by APMC accounting for more than 20 per cent of the total quantity sold in case of soyabean, cotton, arhar and ragi and 19 per cent each in case of groundnut and mung. The share of APMC market in wheat and rapeseed-mustard was 13 per cent each. The cooperatives accounted for 17–25 per cent of the sugarcane delivery with their shares in paddy being only 4–8 per cent and in masoor 6 per cent. The government agencies had significant presence in paddy accounting for 14–18 per cent of total marketed surplus followed by sugarcane, soyabean, and rapeseed-mustard at 6 per cent each. Only cotton and wheat completed with paddy with 15 per cent and 14 per cent, respectively bought by government agencies. The FPOs again did not go beyond 0.1 per cent in most crops with the exception of 0.3 per cent in case of arhar. Similar was the case of contract farming channel which with the exception of sugarcane (7–12 per cent) and paddy (0.7–1 per cent) did not account for even 1 per cent of the total sales. The private processors had a significant share not only in sugarcane (27–34 per cent) but also in arhar (7 per cent), potato (6 per cent), groundnut (12 per cent), soyabean (7 per cent), cotton (5–10 per cent), paddy (8 per cent), and gram (5 per cent). Delayed payment was the major issue only in case of sugarcane.

More surprisingly, with the exception of sugarcane (57 per cent), in most crops, not even 50 per cent farmers were aware of MSP with maximum touching 46 per cent in paddy and 39 per cent in rapeseed and an even smaller percentage of them across crops sold their output at MSP. Other than sugarcane, paddy scored the highest at 24 per cent followed by wheat at 20 per cent and cotton at 18 per cent. The crop insurance scenario was also dismal with only about 25 per cent of soyabean and cotton farmers insuring their crops followed by 20 per cent in jowar, 15 per cent in gram and 11 per cent in paddy besides 17 per cent and 18 per cent each in arhar and mung and 16 per cent in groundnut. This is despite the fact that a very large percentage of households ranging from 22 per cent growing sugarcane to 17 per cent growing mung experienced crop loss due to various reasons (NSO 2021).

It is important to note that the almost landless category of agricultural households had as much total income as the small farmer category which was much higher than those in the submarginal and marginal categories. The income from wages for up to marginal category was higher than income from crop production; overall wage income, on an average, exceeded that from crop production. It was only after one ha. of land possession that crop production income exceeded 50 per cent of the total. Even in case of net farm income, the wage income had a much larger contribution than that from crop production, being almost 33 per cent higher than the latter in the total net income of Rs 8,337 per month. Further, even here the pattern was of almost landless agricultural households' net income exceeding substantially that of the small farmer category and being 1 to 1.5 times that of the submarginal and marginal categories, mainly because of much higher wage income among almost landless agricultural households. Further, there were large variations across states in terms of income from farming. Another important phenomenon to note is that in some states like Andhra Pradesh and Haryana, as much as 35 per cent of the operated holdings were leased in and tenant holdings accounted for 42 per cent and 21 per cent of the total holdings respectively. Even Odisha had a higher leased-in area in total (31 per cent) with 39 per cent tenant holdings compared to Punjab where there was 28 per cent leased-in area with 21 per cent tenant holdings (NSO 2021).

The number of farmers in India has always been a mystery whereas the agricultural census of 2015–16 reported 146.45 million operated holdings. The NSO Survey of 2019 reports 93.09 million agricultural households and 10,198 operational holdings which includes 12.4 million non-agricultural households. This is largely because of the definition of an agricultural household used by the Survey wherein an income of more than Rs 4,000 from crop and animal husbandry and self-employment in agriculture for not less than 30 days during a 6-month period is considered to define agricultural household. It is known that members within a household may operate multiple holdings which are treated separately by agricultural census unlike the Survey which focuses on agricultural households. The state-wise differences in farm income as percentage of agricultural household income is below the all-India average in states like Tamil Nadu, Odisha, and West Bengal while it is much higher than the all-India average (50 per cent) in states like Punjab, Gujarat, Karnataka, Madhya Pradesh, and Bihar (around 60 per cent). It is important to note that the farm income dependence is low (26–44 per cent) when holding size is one ha. or below. But it reaches 70 per cent in the semi-medium category and 90 per cent in the case of large farms. The 50 per cent threshold is crossed for majority of the states when land possessed exceeds one ha. If the criteria of 50 per cent (or more) income from crop and animal husbandry is considered, it brings down the number of agricultural households to just 36 million which is only 39 per cent of the total 93 million agricultural households estimated by the Survey. There are states like Kerala, Jharkhand, and West Bengal, where the percentage of households dependent on farm income in the total is less than 1 per cent while in most other states with the exception of Haryana, their share is higher than the all-India average of 39.1 per cent. In fact, it is the so-called cow belt states which have around 44–49 per cent of the total households being farm income-dependent. There are states like Punjab and Gujarat which have more than 60 per cent of households being farm income-dependent. Still there are others like Karnataka and many of the North East states which have almost 90 per cent of the households being dependent on farm income. Therefore, the argument of household incomes moving away from farm dependence can only be seen as a process of distress diversification. In some states, the percentage of agricultural households earning more than 50 per cent of their income from farming and who have more than 2 ha. of land is just 23 per cent of the total (Damodaran et al. 2021).

It is also important to note that over the last six years (from 2012–13 to 2018–19) when the income from wages and salary has increased from 32.2 per cent to 39.8 per cent, that from cultivation has come down from 47.9 per cent from 37 per cent highlighting the declining role of crop production. However, the share of income from animal farming in monthly household income increased from 11.9 per cent to 15.5 per cent (Table 1.6 and also Chand 2021). Despite the goal of policy being doubling of farmer incomes by 2022, the government launched PM Kisan in 2019 as a direct benefit to landowners at the rate of Rs 6,000 per year which has been outdone by many state governments with more comprehensive and inclusive Direct Benefit Transfers (DBTs) (Table 1.7).

Indian farmers face multiple challenges like excessive stress on water and soil health, lack of knowledge/information about high value/growth products, limited exposure to high productivity practices due to lack of extension (that is, failing to inform and persuade farmers about new technologies and practices and their adoption), inadequate credit access, weak market linkages, and inefficient supply chains. Official recognition of the distress and the agrarian crisis came in the form of an NSO Survey in

**Table 1.6: Source of agricultural household income over the years (percentage of total)**

| *Source* | *2002–03* | *2012–13* | *2018–19#* |
|---|---|---|---|
| Crop production$ | 45.8 | 47.9 | 37* (36.7)** |
| Animal farming | 4.3 | 11.9 | 15.5 (5.3) |
| Wages | 38.7 | 32.2 | 39.8 (48.7) |
| Leasing out of land | – | – | 1.3 (1.6) |
| Non-farm business | 11.2 | 8 | 6 (7.7) |
| **All** | **100** | **100** | **100 (100)** |

*Notes*: * Nominal income (after only paid-out costs deducted).

** Net income after all costs (including imputed) deducted.

# Growth rate in real income over 2002–03 is only 3.4 per cent (CPIAL [Consumer Price Index for Agricultural Labour]) and 5.3 per cent (WPI [Wholesale Price Index]); required was 10.4 per cent growth per annum in real income over 7 years for doubling farmer income (Dalwai committee on DFI).

$ Net income from crop production grew only 1.6 per cent per annum at 2012–13 prices ranging from 0.5 per cent 3 per cent with even negative growth (decline) in some states like Kerala, MP, Odisha, HP, and many NE states.

*Source*: NSO (2021).

2003, which reported that 40 per cent of Indian farmers disliked farming as a profession due to its low profits, high risk, and the lack of social status, and therefore, would like to leave it at the first chance. The higher castes seem to be more disenchanted with farming than SC and ST farmers. Among the SCs and STs, the dislike for farming diminishes with increase in landholding size, whereas it increases with increase in landholding size in the case of other castes (Singh 2018).

The need to focus on farmers' incomes also stems from the fact that a very large proportion of farming households in most of the central and eastern states (23–45 per cent) live below poverty line (BPL), which is higher than the national average (22.5 per cent). The proportion of BPL farming households (17.5–22.5 per cent), even in some of the so-called agriculturally progressive states, such as Gujarat, Karnataka, Maharashtra, and Tamil Nadu, is close to

**Table 1.7: State- and scheme-wise farmer income support programmes in India**

| *State and scheme (year)* | *Annual payment in Rs* | *Share in total household income (per cent) for small and medium farmers* | *Share in total household income (per cent) for small-medium and medium farmers* | *Share in total household income (per cent) for large farmers* |
|---|---|---|---|---|
| Telangana Rythu Bandhu (2018) | 10,000/acre | 25–50 | 72–85 | 324 |
| AP Rythu Bharosa (2019) | 7,500/family incl. sharecropper/tenant | 11–15 | 4–10 | 3 |
| Odisha KALIA (2018) | 4,000/family for S&M farmer and tenant/farm labour | 11–16 | 2–3 | 0.5 |
| WB Krishak Bandhu (2019) | 5,000/farmer/ sharecropper/farm labour | 5–10 | 1–5 | 3 |
| Chhattisgarh RG Kisan Nyay (2020) | 10,000–13,000/acre only for landowners | 15 per cent average for all | | |
| Jharkhand CM Krishi Aashirwad (2018) | 5,000/acre for Kharif season, only for S&M farmers | 16–29 | 4–6 | 8 |
| Haryana CM Parivar Samman Nidhi (2019) | 6,000/family for S&M farmers only and for the landless with <15,000 annual income | 6–12 | 1–5 | 3 |

*Source*: Kavitha et al. 2021.

the national average. Further, the gap between farm and non-farm incomes has grown over the decades, from a ratio of 1:3 in the mid-1980s to 1:4.08 in the middle of the last decade (2004–05), and to 1:3.12 in 2011–12 (Chand 2017).

In this context of agrarian distress and policy goal of increasing farmer incomes, the new channels which include direct purchase, contract farming, and private wholesale markets, besides e-trading, are being allowed by reforming agricultural market laws at state levels through the amendment to the APMC Acts across India, which includes the failed attempt at centralising the reform agenda with Union-level Acts. This volume focuses on regulatory aspects of agricultural markets and their dynamics over two decades (2003–23) in terms of how the regulatory measures have created new space for these emerging channels, and analyses the experience of such measures. This volume does not deal with any policy issue except the MSP issue, which has been a policy issue so far but now there have been demands by the protesting farm unions and many other experts and stakeholders, for the MSP to be made into a legal instrument to protect farmers' interest. The following subsection provides a rationale for regulation in the most debated channel of contract farming, which is being seen as sign of corporatisation of Indian agriculture due to recent reforms including the repealed Acts.

## Rationale for Regulation

The APMC Acts in India were brought in during the 1960s and early 1970s to protect the farmers from private traders and commission agents. These Acts specified the rules of the game for sale and purchase, or even facilitation of any transaction. These Acts have details of various charges which could be levied on sellers and buyers, and even payment rules were specified. Now when the new channels are being allowed to interface with farmers, and as they are larger in scale and are global in many aspects like value chain drivers; multinational and national processors engaging in contract farming; or even supermarkets (both local and global) buying directly from farmers, there is even higher need for regulation of markets and transactions to protect farmers' (small) interests due to the highly unequal bargaining power (Cohen et al. 2021).

The agreements practised across the globe are highly biased (for details of contracts across countries, crops, and agencies, see FAO website at https://www.fao.org/in-action/contract-farming/toolkit/contract-links/en/) and in India, this is even more serious as shown by the clauses of some of the contracts. For example, one potato contract stated: 'The price for Multiplication Rate (MR) lower than expected and agreed shall be decided by the Company which shall be lower than the above-mentioned contract price.'

Further, 'Potatoes shall be graded by Grower prior to delivery at the Grower's discretion, provided that Company shall have the first option to purchase any potatoes stripped by Grower at a price to be negotiated by the parties'.

Another contract by PepsiCo India Holdings (PIH) states: 'PIH will not be held liable or responsible for any failure in the crop or for any shortfall in the yield of the PIH variety potato seeds'. It adds:

> PIH may purchase all or some part of the produce subject to the quality test results. PIH shall neither be liable to take delivery of the multiplied chip grade potatoes from the grower nor shall be liable to pay any consideration for the multiplied chip grade potatoes to the grower if the multiplied chip grade potatoes are not of the quality as is specified in the agreement. However, PIH may at its discretion purchase the rejected potato @Rs 0.5/Kg.

Another potato contract farming player, a multinational subsidiary's contract states: 'If the crop is destroyed under any circumstances or if not appropriate as mentioned in the contract, the producer would be held responsible for it'.

Surprisingly, a local major player in this domain writes in its agreement: 'The farmer agrees to sell his produce to the assigned buyer as per this agreement and can sell to any other buyer if he gets higher price in the market' (Singh 2005, 2012b).

There have been malpractices in supermarket procurement from farmers across various countries including India (Singh 2010, 2011). Similarly, the need for regulation due to many malpractices written into the contracts has also led to international agencies like FAO (Food and Agriculture Organization of the United Nations) and IISD (International Institute for Sustainable Development) (2018) to propagate responsible contracts and contract agreements. There are others which point to legal issues in contract farming and therefore need for regulation (Pultrone 2012).

Globally, there has been such regulation wherever new channels like direct purchase or contract farming became prominent. Speaking specifically of contract farming regulation, France had the Code Rural which makes a written contract farming agreement a must and entails that it should contain certain provisions to ensure that the farmer is aware of the risks and requirements of the agreement. Agrarian Code of Panama also has a provision for contract farming which bars any abusive clauses and mandates certain minimum aspects in a contract agreement. Similarly, Spain has a 2000 law which defines principles of contractual relations and even provides samples of contracts to be agreed upon between parties that are approved of by the Ministry. It mandates prices to be paid, and conditions of payment as well as time and place of delivery, besides dispute resolution method, and provides for a monitoring committee which plays a role in approving the contract agreements (Pultrone 2012).

The Competitive and Fair Agricultural Markets Act of 2006 in the US disallows confidentiality provisions, provides for a cancellation time window without penalty, has provision for damages if the firm breaches the contract besides having a dispute settlement mechanism alongside clear, honest, and accurate terms of the agreement. Thailand and Vietnam both provide for coverage of *force majeure*, compensatory damages, registration of agreements, and a dispute resolution mechanism. The state of Georgia in the US has a poultry grower protection provision during contract negotiation phase, wherein they get a three-day window to review contracts before signing them and three more days after signing to reconsider and cancel it, if needed. Growers also have a right to market price information and being present at the time of weighment of birds (in poultry contract farming) for payment of compensation (Pultrone 2012). In Kenya, though not very desirable, the Dairy Industry Act (1976) gives the Minister of Agriculture the power to set prices and make the Dairy Oversight Board a third party to the contract (Chambers 2015). This is similar to Gujarat in India making APMC as third. party to the contract agreement in its amended APMC Act of 2005, which was later made optional. Kenya has the Sugar Act, which governs contracts between mills and growers, including prescribing a standard contract, and a code of conduct for fresh horticulture sales which guides contracts and suggests fair production practices (Pultrone 2012).

The regulation is needed especially in contract farming as there is generally a lack of clarity in price determination, liability of production loss, and large investment required for contract production, besides termination and confidentiality clauses and environmental damages which may happen to farmer resources. Also, growing monopsony in agribusiness hinders farmer negotiation power and therefore makes them more prone to exploitation (Pultrone 2012).

This volume analyses the regulatory space in the Indian agricultural market domain and its effectiveness from a small producer perspective, and assesses how regulatory oversight has been changing over the decades, with increasing trends towards facilitation and promotion, and less towards regulation, which does not bode well for smallholder interest in increasingly globalised and liberalised markets for farm and allied produce, whether food or fibre. The volume does not examine the ECA and its amended version of 2020 as it is not concerned with the agricultural produce markets directly. Chapter 2 examines the state of affairs at the first attempt of opening up markets through amendment to the APMC Act as a Model Act in 2003, and the Model Agricultural Produce and Livestock Marketing Act of 2017 for its adoption at the state level as advised by the Union government, and its state-level implementation and the variations therein. Also examined is the role and performance of e-NAM as implemented in APMC mandis. Chapter 3 deals with the Model Contract Farming and Services Act, 2018 and the lacunae in this Act, including permitting corporate farming in the disguise of contract farming. Not satisfied with the amendments to the APMC Acts based on the Model Act of 2017 and a separate Model Contract Farming Act of 2018, the Union government enacted central Acts on these two domains which are the subjects of Chapters 4 and 5. Chapter 6 examines the issue of legal guarantee of MSP, as demanded by farmer unions which is still pending despite the agitation being suspended since December 2021. The concluding chapter sums up the discussion on the role of regulation and puts forward some mechanisms for more effective regulation to protect the smallholder interest in new markets, and builds on some of the strengths of the existing marketing system, besides providing for more space for farmer stakeholders like FPOs.

## Notes

1. Under contract farming, what is produced in the farm is as per market requirements; besides, the contracting agencies influence farmer crop choices and practices, and often, such agencies also pick up the produce from the farm and the farmer does not need to go to the mandi

to sell at all. Even direct purchase from farmers by food supermarkets and other buyers under the other new Act of 2020 (also known as APMC mandi bypass Act) also lets buyers go to the farm or very close to it by setting up collection centres to procure, which was previously permitted by the APMCs under the APMC Acts since 2003, but the new Act drove such direct purchase and contract farming outside the purview of the APMC altogether.

2. The e-NAM or the electronic National Agriculture Market is an innovative initiative in agricultural marketing to enhance farmer's accessibility digitally to greater numbers of markets and buyers and to bring transparency in trade transactions. The e-NAM had facilitated online auction of farmer produce to get more buyers placed anywhere to bid on it; it is operated through and from the APMC mandis though it is not mandatory for the APMCs to join the e-NAM. The new laws permitted e-trading across the states and outside the APMCs in the new 'trade area' created by the new law (APMC mandi bypass Act) with no involvement of the APMC.

## References

Chambers, A. 2015. 'Building Enabling Environment for Contract Farming Success', USAID Policy Brief No. 6, February. USAID.

Chand, R. 2017. 'Doubling Farmers' Income– Rationale, Strategy, Prospects and Action Plan', NITI Policy Paper No. 1. New Delhi: NITI Aayog, Government of India.

———. 2021. 'Agriculture in Post Independence India: Looking Back and Looking Ahead', ICAR Lecture Series No. 29, 24 September. New Delhi: NITI Aayog.

Chand, R., P. A. L. Prasanna, and A. Singh. 2011. 'Farm Size and Productivity: Understanding the Strengths of Smallholders and Improving their Livelihoods'. *Economic and Political Weekly* 46(26/27): 5–11.

Cohen, A. J., M. Vicol, and G. Pol. 2021. 'Living Under Value Chains: The New Distributive Contract and Arguments about Unequal Bargaining Power'. *Journal of Agrarian Change*: 1–18.

Damodaran H., M. Krishnamurthy, and S. Agarwal. 2021. 'Agricultural Households and Farming Income: An Initial Analysis of Variations in Income from Farming and Other Sources among Agricultural Households in India', Understanding the Rural Economy series. New Delhi: Centre for Policy Research.

Dev, M. 2012. 'Small Farmers in India: Challenges and Opportunities', IGIDR WP No. 14. Mumbai: IGIDR.

FAO and IISD. 2018. *Model Agreement for Responsible Contract Farming—With Commentary*. Rome: FAO.

Foster, A. D., and M. R. Rosenzweig. 2022. 'Are there Too Many Farms in The World? Labour Market Transaction Costs, Machine Capacities and Optimal Farm Size'. *Journal of Political Economy* 130(3): 636–680.

Gaurav, S., and S. Mishra. 2011. 'Size Class and Returns to Cultivation in India—A Cold Case Reopened', IGIDR Working Paper No. 27. Mumbai: IGIDR.

Harriss-White, B. 2008. 'Introduction: India's Rainfed Agricultural Dystopia'. *The European Journal of Development Research* 20(4): 549–561.

Kavitha, H. N., Pramod Kumar, P. Anbukkani, R. Burman, and P. Prakash. 2021. 'Income Support Schemes: Evaluation of PM KISAN vis-à-vis State Government Schemes'. *Economic and Political Weekly* 56(34): 13–17.

Murphy, S. 2011. *Changing Perspectives: Small Scale Farmers, Markets and Globalization*, Hivos Knowledge Programme Report 2010 (Working Paper). London: IIED and The Hague: Hivos.

NSO (National Statistical Organisation). 2021. *Situation Assessment of Agricultural Households and Land and Livestock Holdings of Households in Rural India, 2019*, NSS 77th Round, September. New Delhi: Ministry of Statistics & Programme Implementation, Government of India.

Pultrone, C. 2012. 'An Overview of Contract Farming: Legal Issues and Challenges'. *Uniform Law Review* 17: 263–289.

Ricciardia, V., N. Ramankuttya, Z. Mehrabia, L. Jarvisa, and B. Chookolingo. 2018. 'How Much of The World's Food do Smallholders Produce?' *Global Food Security* 17: 64–72.

RRA Network and ISB. 2019. *The Rainfed Atlas*. Hyderabad: RRAN and ISB.

Sahan, E., and J. Fischer-Mackey. 2011. 'Making Markets Empower the Poor—Programme Perspectives on Using Markets to Empower Women and Men Living in Poverty', Oxfam Discussion Paper. Oxford: Oxfam GB, November.

SC Committee. 2021. *Report of The Supreme Court Appointed Committee on Farm Laws*, March. New Delhi.

Shankar, P. S. V. 2006. 'Unlocking the Hidden Potential of Dryland Agriculture'. *Seminar* 564, August.

Singh, H. P., K. D. Sharma, G. S. Reddy, and K. L. Sharma. 2004. 'Dryland Agriculture in India'. In Srinivas C. Rao and John Ryan (eds), *Challenges and Strategies of Dryland Agriculture*, Vol. 32, Chapter 6, 67–92, CSSA Special Publications series. Crop Science Society of America, American Society of Agronomy. Available at DOI:10.2135/cssaspecpub32 (accessed July 2023).

Singh, S. 2005. *Political Economy of Contract Farming in India.* New Delhi: Allied Publishers.

———. 2010. 'Implications of FDI in Food Supermarkets'. *Economic and Political Weekly* 45(34): 17–20.

———. 2011. 'FDI in Retail: Misplaced Expectations and Half-truths'. *Economic and Political Weekly* 46(51): 13–16.

———. 2012a. 'Corporate Agribusiness, State and Small Primary Producers in India: Evidence of Exclusion and Potential Innovative Mechanisms for Inclusion', Working Paper 16/2009 under the Collaborative Research Project on Systems of Innovation for Inclusive Development (SIID): Lessons from Rural China and India. New Delhi: CPR.

———. 2012b. *Modern Food Value Chains in India: Emerging Potential for the Poor*. New Delhi: Samskriti.

———. 2018. 'Doubling Farmers' Incomes Mechanisms and Challenges'. *Economic and Political Weekly* 53(7): 15–19.

———. 2021. 'Food Security and Markets: Understanding the Protests over India's Changing Social Contract with Farmers', 15 March, *The Hindu Centre for Politics and Public Policy*. Available at https://www.thehinducentre.com/the-arena/current-issues/article34060554.ece (accessed August 2023).

———. 2022. 'Contextualising the Repealed 2020 Union Agricultural Markets Acts in Farmer Income (Policy) Debate', Prof. V. S. Vyas Memorial Lecture, IDS Jaipur, July.

*The Indian Express*. 2021. 'Farmers end year-long protest: A timeline of how it unfolded', 9 December. Available at https://indianexpress.com/article/india/one-year-of-farm-laws-timeline-7511961/ (accessed August 2023).

van der Ploeg, J. D. 2018. *The New Peasantries: Rural Development in Times of Globalization*. London: Routledge.

Venkateswarlu, J. 2017. *Rainfed Ecosystems in India: A Perspective*. Hyderabad: RRAN and WASSAN.

Vermeulen, S. and L. Cotula. 2010. *Making the Most of Agricultural Investment: A Survey of Business Models that Provide Opportunities for Smallholders*. London: FAO Rome and IIED.

Vijayan, Roshni. 2016. 'Dryland Agriculture in India—Problems And Solutions'. *Asian Journal of Environmental Science* 11(2): 171–177.

Vorley, B., L. Cotula, and M. Chan. 2012. *Tipping the Balance: Policies to Shape Agricultural Investments and Markets in Favour of Small-Scale Farmers*. Research report, IIED London and Oxfam, December.

two

# The Model APMC Acts

## Opening Up Wholesale Markets

Agricultural markets are key to ensuring higher farmer incomes, but in India, agricultural market reforms have been stuck for almost two decades as agriculture is a state subject. Like many other issues related to agriculture, this one too is caught in the tug-of-war between the Union and the state governments, each of which has their own positions and compulsions on carrying out these market reforms. Most of the agricultural produce markets in India are regulated under the state-level APMC (Agricultural Produce Market Committee) Acts though some states do not have any regulation even in the form of APMC Acts. Though the very first regulated market was set up during British rule in 1886 in Hyderabad Presidency, the Royal Commission on Agriculture had recommended the establishment and regulation of agricultural markets and practices only in 1928. Even a bill was prepared for the purpose in 1938 though it could not be converted into an Act. It was only during the 1960s and 1970s that most states enacted APMC Acts and these continued until the early 2000s with some modifications through amendments and relaxations. The APMCs are democratic bodies where stakeholders are represented through elections, and they mobilise their resources through fees and levies for maintenance and development of market infrastructure. Table 2.1 gives state- and union territory-wise penetration of

**Table 2.1: State/UT-wise average area covered by APMC market**

| *Name of the state/UT* | *Area in km²* | *Total no. of regulated PMYs + SMYs* | *Area served by one APMC market in km²* |
|---|---|---|---|
| Andhra Pradesh | 162970 | 191 | 853.25 |
| Arunachal Pradesh | 83743 | 13 | 6442 |
| Assam | 78438 | 226 | 347 |
| Chandigarh | 114 | 1 | 114 |
| Chhattisgarh | 136034 | 187 | 727 |
| Goa | 3702 | 8 | 463 |
| Gujarat | 196024 | 400 | 490 |
| Haryana | 44212 | 281 | 157 |
| Himachal Pradesh | 55673 | 56 | 994 |
| Jammu & Kashmir | 222236 | 25 | 8889 |
| Jharkhand | 79714 | 190 | 420 |
| Karnataka | 191791 | 513 | 374 |
| Madhya Pradesh | 308144 | 545 | 565 |
| Maharashtra | 307713 | 902 | 341 |
| Meghalaya | 22429 | 2 | 11215 |
| Nagaland | 16579 | 19 | 873 |
| Delhi | 1484 | 9 | 165 |
| Odisha | 155707 | 436 | 357 |
| Puducherry | 562 | 8 | |
| Punjab | 50362 | 435 | 116 |
| Rajasthan | 342240 | 454 | 754 |
| Tamil Nadu | 130058 | 283 | 460 |
| Telangana | 114840 | 260 | 442 |
| Tripura | 10493 | 21 | 500 |
| Uttar Pradesh | 240928 | 623 | 387 |
| Uttarakhand | 53484 | 67 | 798 |
| West Bengal | 88752 | 475 | 187 |
| **Total** | **3290840** | **6630** | **496** |

*Notes*: PMY: Primary Market Yards, and SMY: Sub-Market Yards

*Source*: Based on data from LSS (2019).

APMC markets in India and Table 2.2 shows the need for more such markets. However, due to various reasons including poor regulation, the APMCs developed strong vested and rent-seeking interests in many states and did not necessarily protect farmer interest in very many ways (Kumar 2022).

The first attempt at reforms in agricultural markets was made by the Union government with the design of a Model Agricultural Produce Market Committee (APMC) Act in 2003 to advise the states to amend their APMC Acts along its lines. The Model Act provided for new market channels, that is, direct purchase, private wholesale markets, and contract farming for farmers and buyers alike as these were made legal under the Model APMC Act. The other related agricultural market reforms at the Union government level have been the Warehouse Receipt System Act, 2006 and the integrated food law (Food Safety and Standards Act, 2006), besides the amendment to the Companies Act in 2003, under which Farmer Producer Companies (FPCs) were allowed to be set up (Singh 2016).

There is no doubt that agricultural market reforms are much needed and long overdue in light of the changing global and local markets. The emergence of new stakeholders, that is, wholesale 'cash and carry' players; food retail supermarkets (domestic and foreign); online retailers/aggregators; processors; exporters; and farmer producer companies in food and fibre markets has led to new demands on the existing market structures such as APMCs, which most of them are not able to meet as they have not been organised and managed keeping the new players in mind who demand quality produce and consistent supply. These wholesale markets have not changed adequately to meet new (modern retail and consumption) demand in India (unlike Europe where wholesalers supply to supermarkets as third generation markets).

**Table 2.2: State/UT-wise details of average distance in radius between two APMC market yards**

| *Name of the state/UT* | *Total no. of APMC markets (regulated PMYs + SMYs)* | *Distance between two APMC markets in km* |
|---|---|---|
| Andhra Pradesh | 191 | 16.48 |
| Andaman and Nicobar Islands | 0 | 0.00 |
| Arunachal Pradesh | 13 | 45.29 |
| Assam | 226 | 10.51 |
| Bihar | 0 | 0.00 |
| Chandigarh | 1 | 6.03 |
| Chhattisgarh | 187 | 15.22 |
| Goa | 8 | 12.14 |
| Gujarat | 400 | 12.49 |
| Haryana | 281 | 7.07 |
| Himachal Pradesh | 56 | 17.79 |
| Jammu & Kashmir | 25 | 53.21 |
| Jharkhand | 190 | 11.57 |
| Karnataka | 513 | 10.91 |
| Madhya Pradesh | 545 | 13.41 |
| Maharashtra | 902 | 10.42 |
| Meghalaya | 2 | 59.76 |
| Mizoram | 0 | 0.00 |
| Nagaland | 19 | 16.67 |
| Delhi | 9 | 7.25 |
| Odisha | 436 | 10.66 |
| Puducherry | 8 | 0.00 |
| Punjab | 435 | 6.08 |
| Rajasthan | 454 | 15.50 |
| Tamil Nadu | 283 | 12.10 |
| Telangana | 260 | 11.86 |
| Tripura | 21 | 12.62 |
| Uttar Pradesh | 623 | 11.10 |
| Uttarakhand | 67 | 15.94 |
| West Bengal | 475 | 7.72 |
| **Total** | **6630** | **12** |

*Source*: Based on data from LSS (2019).

Thus, it is evident that very less policy attention has been paid to wholesale agricultural produce markets, especially fresh produce (wet) wholesale markets, than needed by state and the APMCs themselves.

Though the existing APMC markets are increasingly being reduced in importance by contract farming and direct purchase arrangements with growers, they are still important for small growers as most of the time, small growers are not preferred as suppliers by contracting agencies and direct-buying fresh produce supermarket retailers (Singh 2013a). This is not to say that the APMC markets (regulated or unregulated) are well-functioning in most cases. In fact, even today, these markets are unable to deliver state-assured Minimum Support Price (MSP) to farmers selling there despite the fact that the state agencies are mandated to procure from these markets. In some states, like Chhattisgarh, even in regulated markets, the farmers, not buyers are still being charged commission by the commission agents which is as per the state APMC Act (information based on field visit in April 2018). Further, fruit and vegetable (F&V) (wholesale or wet) markets are much less effectively regulated than grain markets even in so-called agriculturally advanced states. There are high marketing/transaction costs incurred by the seller farmer due to non-regulation of these markets or poor implementation of the regulations. Finally, there is very little or no appreciation of produce quality even in perishable produce markets, and the problem of chemical residues in such produce has led to enterprising businesses designing and launching an F&V- and meat-washing machine for consumers to remove chemical residue at home after they purchase these produces from the market! The lack of hygiene and convenience is another serious issue as there is very little planning which has gone into setting up of these markets and good agricultural marketing practices (unlike good agricultural practices in farm production sector) are almost unheard of in India.

## APMC Act, 2003 and Competition

In India, the legal reform process started with the Union government enacting the Model Act for State Agricultural Produce Marketing (Development and Regulation) Act, 2003, which allowed three new channels of direct purchase, private wholesale markets, and contract farming besides the APMC mandi, though with permission from the APMC itself. By early 2016, six states (Chhattisgarh, Gujarat, Goa, Karnataka, Mizoram, and Sikkim) had adopted all provisions of the Model APMC Act, and another 12 states (Andhra Pradesh, Arunachal Pradesh, Assam, Haryana, Jharkhand, Madhya Pradesh, Maharashtra, Nagaland, Rajasthan, Telangana, Tripura, and Uttarakhand) only partially amended their APMC Acts but adopted majority of the provisions (ranging from 4–6 out of 7). Only Odisha, Punjab, West Bengal, and Uttar Pradesh had hardly adopted one or two provisions of the Model Act. This amended Act deals with setting up of private markets, selling of produce by growers outside the APMCs (regulated markets); setting up of direct markets and specialised commodity-specific markets; regulation and promotion of contract farming; provision for agencies and measures to promote quality, standards, and alternative markets, and public-private partnerships to facilitate more and better linkage between firms and farmers (GoI 2003b). The amended APMC Act has certain mandatory and optional provisions regarding CF (contract farming) wherein mandatory ones include aspects like who can undertake CF (type of sponsor and of contract grower), details about the land under contract, duration of contract, description of farm produce, other contract specifications like quantity/acreage, entire crop or fixed quantity, produce quality specifications and penalties for lower quality like rejection or lower price, crop delivery arrangements at farm/ factory gate/collection centre, transport arrangements, pricing and credit mechanisms, farmer asset/land indemnity, compulsory registration of contracts with the local authority, and the procedure for dispute resolution. On the other hand, the optional features include those relating to farm practices, joint crop insurance, support services to be provided, farmer-management forum for monitoring of contract system performance, and monitoring of quality and yields.

An assessment (CUTS 2016) of the Model APMC Act, 2003 from a competition angle argues that the APMC structure does not seem to effectively prevent anti-competitive conduct like cartels among buyers. Further, there is scope for interference by local politicians in the regulatory structure which can affect the free flow of goods. In fact, the Model Act also allows interference of state governments in the regulatory mechanism. Though the Act allows for setting up of private markets, the conditions for obtaining licence like minimum five ha. of land for setting up the private market yard make this channel trade-restrictive and anti-competitive. It also creates a conflict of interest as the APMC market with which the private market may compete is the agency to issue a licence and monitor its functioning and this has an adverse effect on competition. Therefore, the assessment concludes that the Model Act of 2003 does not seem relevant for the present-day agricultural market dynamics and hence, is not good enough to be advocated as a starting point for agricultural market reform. It fails to recognise the principle that competition among the buyers of agricultural produce would benefit the farmers (sellers) most. Rather, it tends to discourage farmers holding or controlling a bigger portion of the value chain, including reaching consumers directly. In fact, it states

> In sum, the very soul of APMC Acts including the model APMC Act is anticompetitive in nature and hence requires change of orientation with stated objective of engendering competition among the buyers of agricultural produce. This would be in the best interest of the farmers if it is the aim of agricultural market regulatory regime (CUTS 2016: 4).

The assessment further goes on to say that the Act needs to be pro-competitive in design yet permitting certain restrictive clauses to achieve targeted objectives, if required. It argues that bidding may have been responsible for better price realisation in earlier times. Today, in this ICT (Information and Communications Technology) era, the price realisation does not happen due to bidding. Now, the prices are known and published prior to the bidding process. Therefore, the whole arrangement of APMC does not present a system where price realisation happens through a competitive process. It identifies clauses on definition of agricultural produce, agriculturist, business, processing, retail sale, and trader, as provisions which create entry barriers and cause adverse effect on competition and restrict the freedom of players in the market. It even questions the composition of the market committee as highly bureaucratic, political, and unprofessional, leading to local politicians making their way into the regulatory system in the name of farmers and colluding with local traders who fund them during elections which makes the process not only anti-competitive but also anti-farmer. The assessment thus argues that the Model Act discourages farmers from undertaking multiple roles in agricultural value chains, unlike other entities.

The assessment even questions the provision for public-private partnerships (PPPs) in management and development of market infrastructure as it could lead to making these PPP entities monopolist, which may result in imposing unfair conditions on farmers. Even the provision of publishing and circulating data on arrivals and prices in the market brought for sale is found to be problematic by the assessment as it may lead to cartelisation among buyers. In fact, it notes 'complete transparency is not always good especially if market is conducive for cartelization' (CUTS 2016, 10). Even the exemption of commercial transactions between two traders from the purview of APMC regulation is not without its challenges since it can lead to cartelisation and help vested (private) interests. The application of market fee is also found to be limiting free and fair market processes and the Economic Survey 2014–15 is cited to say that such a market fee acts as a major impediment to create a national common market in agricultural commodities. The requirement of various operators to register with the APMC is seen as creating entry barriers, and promoting cartelisation and conflict of interest. The assessment recommends a complete repeal of the APMC Acts, or in case amendments are instituted, it recommends doing away with all restrictions with respect to sale and purchase of agricultural produce vis-à-vis the APMC-operated markets. It recommends

> the amended law should leave APMC operated market as mere one of the players amongst many. Let the regulated markets compete with emerging (non-APMC regulated) private markets. But the law should be such that anybody should be free to sell to anybody at any place (CUTS 2016: 17).

The Model contract farming agreement (under APMC Act) is quite fair in terms of sharing of costs and risks between the sponsor and the grower (GoI 2003a). But, it leaves out many aspects of farmer interest protection like delayed payments and deliveries, contract cancellation damages if producer has made firm-specific heavy investments, inducement/force/intimidation to enter a contract, disclosure of material risks, competitive performance-based payments, and sharing of production risks. Also, there are state-level variations in the amended Acts as agriculture is a state subject in India. For example, in Gujarat, the amended Act makes the APMC a party in the tripartite contract (involving the farmers, the contract agency, and the APMC; earlier it was mandatory if contracting agency used any APMC facility, but now it is optional) stating the logic that APMCs have a useful role as facilitator as they have a long-standing relationship with farmers, and can disseminate the contract farming concept and practice as well as monitor the latter. Though the Union Model Act exempts contract procurement from market fee, the Gujarat Act makes it mandatory to pay the prescribed cess to the concerned APMC or in case of multi-location operations, to the Gujarat State Agricultural Marketing Board (GSAMB) which will apportion it to the concerned APMCs. Haryana (15 per cent of the value of produce) and Gujarat (5 per cent of the value of produce) also prescribe bank guarantees for preventing defaults by contracting agencies. On the other hand, Bihar has abolished the APMC Act instead of amending it and that makes the agricultural market in the state totally unregulated.

Further, in Haryana, contract price was deemed to not be less than the previous year's MSP of crop, if applicable. In Gujarat, only processors and exporters were eligible to purchase the commodity from the farmer, which was grown under contract farming scheme, provided that the concerned person furnished information or proof of such certificate of registration of such agreement given by GSAMB to the concerned APMC.

On the other hand, Punjab instead of permitting contract farming through the APMC, enacted a separate Contract Farming Act, 2013 with the provision of a contract farming commission having a CCFC (Chief Contract Farming Commissioner) and CFCs (Contract Farming Commissioners).

## Punjab's (Repealed) Separate Contract Farming Act, 2013

Punjab had not adequately amended the APMC Act by 2013, when it framed a separate Act on CF, instead of providing for it under the APMC Act (which was amended only in 2017). Many other states amended their APMC Acts to provide for CF. The major reason for Punjab going for a separate Act on CF can be found in the political economy of the state's agribusiness sector, wherein farming and trading interests have been at loggerheads in protecting their interests until recently. There was a constant battle between the two lobbies on direct payments by buying agencies to farmers for their produce, and the issue was unresolved for the last decade. Whereas the farmer lobby wanted direct payments, the *arthiya*[1] lobby opposed it vehemently. Direct payments hit the business of interlocking of credit, input, and output markets run by arthiyas in which a *parchi* (slip) system prevails for lending in kind to farmers and recovery of payments at the time of sale of produce.

Direct purchases (when permitted with the APMC Act amendment) would have reduced volumes in APMC mandis and, therefore, arthiyas' and traders' hold on farmer produce. Furthermore, private wholesale markets (again under the APMC Act amendment) would have created competition for arthiyas/ traders operating from APMC mandis and for the Mandi Board itself. This was perhaps the reason that instead of amending the APMC Act, which would have involved allowing direct purchases and setting up of private wholesale markets, besides permitting

CF and, therefore, adversely affecting the arthiyas and the Mandi Board; the separate CF Act route was taken.

In the Punjab Act, only temporary structures on a farmer's land for the duration of the contract could be put up by the buyer, and if these were not removed immediately after the expiry of the contract, these were to become the property of the producer. No recoveries of any dues or penalties could be made from the producer by way of sale or mortgage of his/her contracted land. This provision was in line with the Model APMC Act and removed fears about contracting companies staking claims on contract growers' land.

The district collector was to be responsible for CF dispute resolution and give a decision within 30 days, and no civil court could consider such cases. Decisions of the collector were to be like a decree of the court. A contracting party could appeal after payment of 50 per cent of dues of the disputed amount. Buyers and farmers were to be subject to prison terms and fines for violations of the Act, or failures to correct violations after conviction.

There were many missing elements in the Punjab Act, as well as some anomalies. For example, notified crops in the Act also included gur, shakkar, and khandsari, which are generally not contract-produced, as they are value-added products from sugarcane. It seemed the list of crops was obtained from the state agricultural marketing board which had been notified under the APMC Act. But, all crops/produce on this list would not be amenable to being produced under CF (Singh 2013b).

## Role of e-NAM

The electronic National Agriculture Market (e-NAM) initiative started in 2015 and had 585 markets linked to this platform by

2018. The main purpose of this initiative was to discover more competitive auction prices with the participation of more buyers from across the country who can bid for produce in the local APMC market (Reddy and Neh 2019; Singh 2019). The e-NAM electronic trading portal that networks existing APMC markets across India is managed by SFAC (Small Farmers' Agri-Business Consortium) as the lead implementing agency for e-NAM. The e-NAM is a virtual market but has a physical market at the back end. The performance of this initiative remains mixed as shown by various studies. The e-NAM initiative was approved with a budget of Rs 200 crore in July 2015 for setting up e-platforms in 585 select wholesale (APMC) markets. The Union government provided the software free of cost along with Rs 30 lakh per mandi for setting up the required infrastructure. Table 2.3 shows the state/UT-wise spread of e-NAM till March 2018. By May 2020, 1000 mandis across 21 states and UTs were integrated with Rs 1.68 crore registered farmers and trade of the order of Rs 1.14 lakh crore was carried out through e-NAM (Bhattacharya and Chowdhury 2021) (Table 2.3).

A study of e-NAM in Karnataka and Maharashtra to assess the adequacy of marketing infrastructure for it outlined that the main objectives of the e-NAM were: to integrate markets at the state level and eventually across the states, to streamline transaction procedures uniformly across all markets to promote efficiency, to promote better marketing opportunities for farmers by providing online access to more buyers, to establish quality assaying systems for quality assurance, and to promote stable prices and availability of quality produce to consumers. The field assessment found that sales payments were still being made to farmers in cash by the commission agents. Further, assaying facility was mostly used by trader exporters while local traders preferred visual inspection.

**Table 2.3: State/UT-wise spread of e-NAM by March 2018**

| *State* | *Markets integrated* | *Farmers registered* | *Farmers participated in trade on e-NAM* |
|---|---|---|---|
| Andhra Pradesh | 22 | 741164 | 536701 |
| Chandigarh | 1 | 2483 | 1812 |
| Chhattisgarh | 14 | 92982 | 76817 |
| Gujarat | 79 | 620563 | 330954 |
| Haryana | 54 | 2133288 | 1412225 |
| Himachal Pradesh | 19 | 75322 | 52166 |
| Jharkhand | 19 | 16963 | 1419 |
| Madhya Pradesh | 58 | 1371473 | 360343 |
| Maharashtra | 60 | 421241 | 78738 |
| Odisha | 10 | 37372 | 5867 |
| Puducherry* | 2 | 801 | 677 |
| Punjab* | 19 | 2900 | 887 |
| Rajasthan | 25 | 747605 | 265259 |
| Tamil Nadu | 23 | 101741 | 15119 |
| Telangana | 47 | 1295569 | 1006087 |
| Uttar Pradesh | 100 | 2852161 | 373486 |
| Uttarakhand | 16 | 15674 | 6662 |
| West Bengal* | 17 | 2295 | 151 |
| **Total** | **585** | **10531597** | **4525370** |

*Note*: *Markets integrated recently in March 2018.
*Source*: Based on data from LSS (2019).

In Karnataka, 22 lakh farmers were registered with the Unified Market Platform (UMP). So far as the status of market infrastructure is concerned, of the total of 513 markets in Karnataka across four divisions, it was revealed that of the 134 APMC markets, 63 needed godown facilities and 104 required covered auction platform. On the other hand, in Maharashtra of the 292 APMCs, 206 had godowns, 208 had auction platforms, and 160 had weighing scales, 86 required godowns, 84 needed covered auction platforms, 250 required assay labs, and 208 required cattle sheds. The unit cost for enabling e-trading at the APMC level was Rs 10 lakh. The study pointed out that since more than 50 per cent of the marketing surplus was traded through the APMC, APMC reform was a part of the solution (NABARD 2018).

It was found that the implementation of the UMP in Karnataka in 2014 led to an average 5.1 per cent, 3.6 per cent, and 3.5 per cent increase in the modal prices of paddy, groundnut, and maize, and generated higher benefit only for those farmers who produce higher quality commodities. Given the low profit margins of small farmers, ranging from 2–9 per cent, this meant an increase in the profit from 36 per cent to 159 per cent but UMP had no statistically significant impact on modal prices of cotton, green gram, or tur (Levi et al. 2020). This shows that such interventions work in some commodity markets and not in others. Even in the case of higher quality production, only cotton benefitted and not groundnut. It was found that paddy, groundnut, and cotton were quality-sensitive commodity in terms of their prices, whereas prices of maize was less sensitive due to its use predominately as cattle feed. The coefficient of variation of three commodities was much higher than that of maize. The high impact group of crops differs from others mainly due to logistic challenge for cross-market trading, higher efficiency bidding under UMP, the level of in-market concentration of a commodity, and the price discovery process used.

The major issues in e-NAM markets include: trader/commission agent (CA or arthiya) resistance (35–75 per cent of both CAs and traders) stemming from higher competition for them and interlocked transactions for credit recovery becoming difficult as e-payments are made to farmers in e-NAM, lack of quality assessment for distant buyers, traders still preferring manual quality check (Pavithra et al. 2018), delayed payments, poor connectivity, lack of guidance on e-processes, traders being less enthused than farmers, and poor grading and storage infrastructure (Sekhar and Bhatt 2018). Further, due to e-NAM, price volatility increased and decreased in the same commodities (like paddy, potato, tomato, and onion) across different markets, for example, in Haryana. Moreover, there was higher price realisation only in paddy, bajra, and cotton in post–e-NAM period in e-NAM channel which was used for price information, sale, and payment by both farmers and traders (ibid.).

Yet, another study of e-NAM in Uttarakhand (Agarwal et al. 2019) found that only 2.6 per cent to 11.8 per cent of all farmers across various mandis studied were registered under the e-NAM though number of registered traders and commission agents were higher at 15–150 per cent of all registered CAs and traders across mandis as traders from other places in India could register under e-NAM in any APMC. Further, farmer awareness of e-NAM was the lowest at 45 per cent compared with awareness of farmers about other channels of marketing like contract farming, direct purchase, or farmer-consumer market yard (FCMY), though all the traders and CAs were aware of all the channels.

A study of the role of e-NAM (Bhattacharya and Chowdhury 2021) in integrating agricultural commodity market in terms of prices in the context of onion for the major markets of Maharashtra, Karnataka, Rajasthan, and West Bengal during the pre–e-NAM period (2010–16) and post–e-NAM period (2016–19) found some evidence of such market integration although multiple factors were found to govern onion prices before the introduction of e-NAM. However, the study did not mention how many of the onion markets had e-NAM facility across the states. The onion prices on an average were the highest in West Bengal and the lowest in Rajasthan in pre–e-NAM period. This continued to be the case even during the post–e-NAM period with the highest volatility in onion prices in West Bengal both during pre- and post–e-NAM period. In the post–e-NAM period, onion prices of India were positively related to the prices in Maharashtra, Karnataka, and Rajasthan. On the other hand, prices of onion in West Bengal were negatively and significantly related to all-India prices for the same (ibid.). It was argued that to make a difference, the e-NAM should have achieved 50 per cent of the total volume of commodities traded in APMCs by 2020 (Acharya 2017). However, the e-NAM coverage was nowhere near this figure as at the beginning of 2020, only 360 out of the 585 e-NAM APMC mandis were conducting online transactions (Nuthalapati et al. 2022). Another study of e-NAM across six states (Uttar Pradesh, Madhya Pradesh, Haryana, Maharashtra, Telangana, and Gujarat) found that the farmers who participated (mostly with irrigation) obtained 3.75 per cent higher prices in these markets vis-à-vis the prices received before selling to these markets (ibid.).

The above assessment of the reforms in APMC market system across states shows that though states were on the path to open up markets by and large, some states lagged behind for political economy reasons while others had their own perspectives on how far they should go in opening up markets for agricultural produce to different types of buyers through different channels.

## The Model APLM Act, 2017: Regulation or Facilitation?

After more than 14 years of struggle by the Union Ministry of Agriculture and Farmer Welfare (MoAFW) to get the Model APMC Act, 2003 accepted at the state level, which was only adopted by some states fully, some others only partially, whereas a few states are still not looking at it (for example, Uttar Pradesh); the MoAFW has come up with another Model Act—Agricultural

Produce and Livestock Marketing (Promotion and Facilitation) Act, 2017 (hereafter APLMA 2017), which was supposed to be more in tune with the changing times. It had also decided to take contract farming out of the APMC domain citing conflict of interest which was not letting the contract farming practice spread, as traders and commission agents oppose it due to their business getting adversely affected as the contracted produce does not have to come to the APMC mandi and does not need to pass through the mandi agents. Therefore, taking a hint from Punjab, a Model Agricultural Produce and Livestock Contract Farming and Services (Promotion and Facilitation) Act, 2018 (hereafter APLCFSA 2018) was floated by the MoAFW which is on the lines of the Punjab Contract Farming Act, 2013 which was never operationalised (Singh 2013b). The new Model APLCFSA 2018 also mentions that one of the benefits of keeping contract farming and services out of the purview of the APMC would be that the buyers would not need to pay the market fee and commission charges resulting in a saving of 5–10 per cent of their transaction costs (MoAFW 2018: v).

## *Major Conceptual, Policy, and Governance Issues in Model APLMA, 2017*[2]

The fact that the Model Act reflects a major policy change is seen in the very title of the Act which is called APLM (Promotion and Facilitation) Act 2017. The title seems to suggest that there is no need for regulation anymore and that farmers do not need protection in markets.

The Model APLMA retains the direct purchase from farmers (outside the APMC mandi) provision like the 2003 version, but unlike the 2003 Act which allowed contract farming within its ambit, the 2017 Act does not deal with the contract farming channel as the 2017 Union budget announced the enactment of a separate Contract Farming (CF) Act which has been already designed and circulated as stated earlier.

The other non-starter provision in the 2003 Act—private wholesale markets (other than APMC markets) are still retained in the Model Act. Why this is not taken out of the purview of the APMC Act is not clear as there is even bigger conflict of interest in this than in contract farming, as shown by the experience of the last 15 years. This is so because these private markets would compete directly with the APMC market for buyers and sellers. This was evident in the case of private wholesale markets under the previous Act of 2003 where not many private markets could come up as the local APMCs felt threatened by them and scuttled them by not allocating land, placing other conditions, and even charging a fee from them, despite many of them being granted licences. On the other hand, there is at least some amount of contract farming being practised in most states. Additionally, the 2017 Act introduces e-trading and farmer-consumer market yard (FCMY), both by APMC and private parties; market sub-yard (different from sub-market yard); market of national importance (MNI); special commodity markets (SCM) for crops like F&V, flowers, cotton, medicinal and aromatic plants; livestock markets like camel markets; and Farmer Producer Company (FPC) as a new entity/mechanism. Through these, it expands the scope of agricultural markets and their regulation, and rightly so. In fact, even a 'street' can be declared a market under the Model Act.

On p. 1 (MoAFW 2017), the draft mentions the objective of the Act: 'to give freedom to the agriculturists to sell their produce across time and space'. While this is a well-meaning statement but the question arises: Why is such a freedom not needed for buyers to buy farm produce? On the other hand, a new category of adhoc buyer has been included without any rationale being provided for such a provision. A new concept of 'overtrading' has been introduced, which refers to a trader handling more than the amount of produce/livestock for which he has provided security or bank guarantee to the APLMC. Surprisingly, throughout the Act, the seller and the buyer are addressed as he/him which is gender insensitive and unfair to women farmers, women sellers, and women buyers, given that now India has many women farmers (with 15 per cent land titles being with women) and groups of women farmers like Kudumbashree in Kerala. Further, commission agent is defined as one who buys or sells agricultural produce on behalf of his principal. This is conceptually wrong as CAs work on commission basis and cannot buy unless they are licensed and cannot hold/control such produce as they do not take title to goods by definition. In fact, a trader is also defined as an agent (p. 10–11) which shows a lack of basic conceptual clarity.

Unfortunately, the Act still defines CA as someone who would collect payment and pay to the seller. This is startling for an Act of 2017 to propose, as it is not clear what logic there could be in not paying the seller directly for her produce. This, despite the fact that the issue of direct payments to farmers for their produce was hanging fire for the last 15 years in Punjab and was resolved just before the repealed 2022 farm Acts came in. This is a very regressive step in the Act and perhaps reflects the political economy of agricultural markets in India where the CAs have acquired political clout, and the state governments are not able and willing to protect the interests of the primary stakeholder of such markets, that is, the farmers. Central agencies like the FCI (Food Corporation of India) were eager to pay directly to farmers but it was the state governments (e.g., Punjab) which did not want this to happen! This was so because there was serious interlocking of output and credit and output and input markets where the CAs also engaged in moneylending to farmers informally (and illegally) and wanted their repayment to be recovered through this mode of indirect payments to farmers by public and private buying agencies.

The biggest change in the domain of APMC as per the Model APLMA, 2017 is that it would not regulate marketing of notified agricultural produce in its delineated market area, but only in principal, sub-market and market sub-yards. Here, the issue then is: Who would regulate direct purchase outside the market yard by direct buyers like food supermarkets or traders or exporters? Even if market fee has to be collected on such produce (which is recommended to be one-fourth of the applicable market fee), how would that be recorded, monitored, and verified? This is also contradictory to Section 4(1) of the Act which declares the whole state as one unified market. If this unified market is still to be regulated for the benefit of farmer as seller and for fair play for all involved, who would do it as the APMC has no jurisdiction outside the principal market yard, sub-market yard and market sub-yard?

Further, other than in the name of the Act and in defining what livestock means (cows, buffaloes, bullocks, bulls, goat, and sheep; also poultry, fish, and such other animals and products thereof specified in the schedule), it does not deal with this very important sector of the agribusiness economy, where issues of quality, hygiene, and food safety are of a very serious nature in terms of health as well as global markets. By clubbing the farm produce and livestock into one legislation, it also fails to recognise that the dynamics of these markets are very different in terms of perishability as well as frequency and nature of transactions.

The Act also defines APMC as a government/administration agency like the agricultural marketing board, which is not desirable; after all, how can a body which is made up of elected members from different stakeholders be called a government agency? The

Act recognises only the agricultural marketing board. What about states which have only agricultural marketing departments like Andhra Pradesh or Telangana? This shows that the Act has not provided for the existing diversity of marketing arrangements and institutions across Indian states. The State Agricultural Marketing Board (SAMB) would have only representatives from Producer Companies. It is not clear why cooperatives which have been around for so long, are not given this space. Supersession of the APMC by Director, Marketing remains as in the old Act.

## *APLM Governance, Farmer Interest Protection, and Market Fee*

All agricultural markets are for farmers and buyers who are the primary stakeholders in them. Surprisingly, there is no farmer representation in the Market of National Importance (MNI) Executive Committee unlike the APLMC. Further, though there is so much policy focus on Farmer Producer Companies (FPCs), there is no FPC representation in APLMC with only cooperative marketing societies being given some space. This is despite the fact that in 2012, the Ministry had issued a notification to all state governments to treat FPCs as equal to cooperatives for all policy purposes. Further, though APLMC markets are mostly located at taluka level, there is no provision for a member from Panchayat Samiti. Only Zila Parishad and Gram Panchayat have been given representation in APLMC markets though the first APLMC would have a representative from a local authority (such as Panchayat Samiti or Zila Parishad or municipal committee or corporation). The first APLMC would have only one member from a cooperative marketing society besides 10 agriculturist members, two of whom would be chair and vice chair. Here again, representation from FPCs is missing. Further, the Act states that the Executive

Committee (EC) would hold office till the pleasure of the government/administration and this can cause damage to the democratic functioning of the APLMCs as they can be superseded anytime by political and bureaucratic stakeholders for reasons not in the interest of the APLMC and its real stakeholders.

More problematically, why approval of Director, Marketing/ Managing Director (MD) of State Agricultural Marketing Board for every infrastructure investment like godowns, storage, and farm input stocking and borrowing is required is not clear. It can create hurdles in the development and functioning of the APLMC markets and create opportunities for rent-seeking. In some states, the agricultural markets are under the agricultural department and this can lead to conflict between the departments as Director (Marketing) would be from another department.

Finally, the Act is biased in favour of farmers in the structure of the APMC committee as it allows an agriculturist to be a member of a second APMC if he has sold produce in it at least once in the last one year or five times in the last five years. Why allow such dual membership when traders, CAs, and others like weighmen and *hammals*[3] are allowed only one APMC membership as voters?

A maximum commission of 2 per cent of the value of produce on non-perishable and a maximum of 4 per cent of perishable produce value, including all expenses incurred by CA on storage and other services is provided for in the Model Act. On the other hand, the APLMC fee would be not more than 2 per cent of non-perishable produce value and not more than 1 per cent of perishable produce value (MoAFW 2017: 57–58). It is difficult to understand why a lower fee on perishables is recommended when there is a higher CA commission on perishable produce which is anyway high-value. The market fee and commission between two types of produce are mutually inconsistent, but no logic is provided anywhere for this differentiation.

Some of the processes specified would make market regulation more efficient, for example, the provision that licence is to be granted/renewed/refused within 10 days of application and after that it would be granted/renewed automatically. Further, all existing licences would be automatically converted into single-state licences after the new Act and before that, they would be deemed to be statewide licences. Even the private wholesale market committee trade licencees can apply for conversion into statewide licences. But, it also states that there would be no consideration of domicile, purchase/collection centre or minimal purchase requirement for renewal of licence. This sounds a bit strange as when the licence is granted by an APLMC, it should be renewed by the APLMC alone so that there is some record of renewal of licences. Even more problematic is the provision that the State Director of Agricultural Marketing would give nationwide inter-state trading licence. The question which arises from this provision is: How can s/he give it when the domain of such official is only that state in which s/he is serving? This is likely to cause problems as this undermines the autonomy of the state in terms of another state's official giving licences in its territory.

The Model APLMA for the first time mandates the APLMC to take measures to prevent sale/purchase of produce below Minimum Support Price (MSP) in APLM market, if applicable (MoAFW 2017: 40). But, this is not a fair provision as the MSP is promised by the government, and not private trade. Therefore, forcing the private trade to buy produce at or above MSP or penalising them for not doing so can kill the private markets for agricultural produce. Maharashtra, which tried to bring this into its APLM Act, had to withdraw this provision due to traders' strike in 2018.

The Act also provides for payment to the farmer seller (in APLM or direct purchase) on the same day. Otherwise, there could be seizure of the produce of the buyer. This is a new and welcome provision as delayed payments can cause plenty of trouble for farmer sellers whether under APLM, or in direct sale to buyers. It also mentions at another place (MoAFW 2017: 56) that the buyer would have to make an additional payment of 1 per cent of the total produce value per day upto five days for late payment for the bought produce, after which there could be cancellation of licence for one year. This good provision is borrowed from the Rajasthan APMC Act.

There are also penalties for non-payment of fees/user charges but they are only upto five times or a maximum of Rs 10,000 which is not a very effective deterrent. The Model Act provides for the APLMC to ensure that traders do not hoard produce but no measures to prevent it are specified. This, therefore, is a half-hearted provision as no implications are mentioned for the party involved or the APLMC.

The Act also provides for the APLMC to publicise benefits of regulation so that farmers and buyers are not taken for a ride. That is likely to improve marketing efficiency and reduce cost and improve realisation for all stakeholders. For the first time, the Model Act provides for public-private partnership at the APLMC level. This is important as it provides for engagement of the elected body with private entities for local-level infrastructure and facilities development and their management, which can help professionalisation of APLMCs and their operations.

### *Private Markets and Direct Purchase: Regulation or Promotion?*

The Act imposes a ceiling on private market yard user charges by the government, which perhaps is to protect the private player from excessive charges which may act as a disincentive for investment in such markets. Further, the private wholesale markets would contribute to a revolving Marketing Development Fund (MDF, maintained by Director, Marketing) from user charges at the same rate as the traditional APMC market. Even private parties can set up FCMYs, but limits on consumer purchase to call it retail purchase are specified. Whether such markets are only for perishables or non-perishables too is not clear. The private market player would pay a licence fee and bank guarantee for the private market yard, or FCMY as prescribed. It would not charge any fees from one set of users, that is, farmer sellers. Farmers can sell directly to consumers in FCMYs, and warehouses, cold storages and other such structures would fall under market sub-yard category. No user charges can be levied on farmer sellers in direct purchase in a declared market sub-yard or when direct purchase happens at farm-level.

The food retail supermarkets, processors, exporters and bulk buyers (which, it is hoped, would include not known if it includes farmer producer companies) are allowed to purchase directly from farmers. They are to pay 0.25 per cent of the applicable market fee on their wholesale purchases within seven days into an MDF. Essential Commodities Act (ECA) would not apply on these players upto their annual capacity. Some states already feel that this fee is too low to maintain physical marketing infrastructure used by such buyers like roads, bridges and the like. They are even opposed to a one-time levy of market fee within a state despite the produce going to several markets on the ground that since market infrastructure is being used again and again by the same buyer/ trader, why should it not pay market fee each time as it is using services of the market provider?

The F&V sold outside market yards are exempted from market fee and are not to be regulated under the 2017 Act. A legitimate question which arises is: why not extend the same treatment to non-perishables? Most disappointingly, the Act ignores the important and vexed issue of the role of arthiyas in the APMCs and maintains them as central agents in the system despite good practices like abolition of CAs in Madhya Pradesh in 1985.

The foregoing analysis of the various provisions of the Model Act reveals that it is more about facilitation and not enough for regulation to protect farmer interest. Besides, it fails to come up to the required level of dynamism in agricultural markets necessary for the twenty-first century.

## Notes

1. Arthiyas are commission agents (CAs) and traders licensed by the APMC under the APMC Act. The commission agent known as *kachcha* arthiya is only an agent who facilitates transaction between the farmer and the buyer for a commission specified in the Act, mostly from the buyer, whereas, *pucca* arthiya also buys farm produce directly from farmers. Some of them have both of these licences.
2. This section was published earlier in 2018 as part of an article by the author in the *Economic and Political Weekly* titled 'Reforming Agricultural Markets in India: A Tale of Two Model Acts' (Singh 2018), and has been reproduced here with permission.
3. 'Hammal' refers to a labourer or coolie engaged in *dara-making* ('dara' stands for 'heap' in Punjabi), loading, unloading, filling, stitching, emptying, or carrying any agricultural produce in the notified market area (MoAFW 2017).

## References

Acharya, S. 2017. 'Effective Implementation of Agricultural Price and Marketing Policy for Doubling Farmers' Incomes: Doable Priority Actions'. *Agricultural Economics Research Review* 30: 1–12.

Agarwal, P., R. Singh, and O. P. Singh. 2019. 'New Agricultural Marketing System: Awareness, Status, Perceptions and Impact in Uttarakhand'. *Indian Journal of Agricultural Marketing* 33(1): 44–53.

Bhattacharya, R., and S. Chowdhury. 2021. 'How Effective is e-NAM in Integrating Food Commodity Prices in India? Evidence From Onion Market', NIPFP WP 336. New Delhi: NIPFP.

CUTS (Consumer Unity & Trust Society). 2016. *Competition Assessment Model APMC Act 2003*. Jaipur: CUTS. Available at https://cuts-ccier.org/pdf/competition-assessment-of-model-apmc-act-2003-for-the-cci.pdf (accessed August 2023).

GoI (Government of India). 2003a. *Contract Farming Agreement and its Model Specifications*, 17 September. New Delhi: Ministry of Agriculture, Department of Agriculture and Co-operation, Krishi Bhawan.

———. 2003b. *The Model State Agricultural Produce Marketing (Development & Regulation) Act, 2003*, September. MoAFW, Government of India.

Kumar, T. N. 2022. *Farmers, Farm Laws and Ways Forward*. Report for the Food and Land Use Coalition India, New Delhi.

Levi, R., M. Rajan, S. Singhvi, and Y. Zheng. 2020. 'The Impact of Unifying Agricultural Wholesale Markets on Prices and Farmers' Profitability' *PNAS* 117(5): 2366–71.

LSS (Lok Sabha Secretariat). 2019. *Agriculture Marketing and Role of Weekly Gramin Haats*, Standing Committee on Agriculture, Report 62, 3 January.

MoAFW (Ministry of Agriculture & Farmers' Welfare). 2017. *Model Act* [*The State/UT Agricultural Produce and Livestock Marketing (Promotion and Facilitation) Act, 2017*], April. New Delhi: MoAFW, Department of Agriculture, Co-operation and Farmers' Welfare, Government of India.

———. 2018. *Model Act* [*The State/UT Agricultural Produce and Livestock Contract Farming and Services (Promotion and Facilitation) Act, 2018*], February. New Delhi: MoAFW, Department of Agriculture, Co-operation and Farmers' Welfare, Government of India.

NABARD. 2018. *Status of Marketing Infrastructure under Electronic National Agriculture Markets: A Quick Study*. Mumbai: NABARD.

Nuthalapati, C. S. R., Y. Bhatt, and S. K. Beero. 2022. 'Is the Electronic Market the Way Forward to Overcome Market Failures in Agriculture?' *Economic and Political Weekly* 57(41): 52–60.

Pavithra S., C. P. Gracy, R. Saxena, and G. G. Patil. 2018. 'Innovations in Agricultural marketing: A Case Study of e-Tendering System in Karnataka, India'. *Agricultural Economics Research Review* 31(1): 53–64.

Reddy, A. A., and Mehjbeen Neh. 2019. 'Electronic National Agricultural Markets, Impacts, Problems and Way Forward'. *IIM Kozhikode Society & Management Review* 8(2): 143–155.

Sekhar, C. S. C., and Y. Bhatt. 2018. 'Electronic National Agricultural Market (E-NAM): A Review of Performance and Prospects in Haryana'. Delhi: Agricultural Economics Research Centre, University of Delhi.

Sekhar, C. S. C., A. Tripathi, and Y. Bhatt. 2018. 'Ensuring MSP to Farmers: Are Deficiency Payment an Option'. *Economic and Political Weekly* 53(51): 50–57.

Singh, S. 2013a. 'The Practice of Contract Farming in India: Making it Inclusive and Effective'. *Food Chain* 3(3): 137–154.

———. 2013b. 'Regulating Contract Farming—Punjab Way', *The Tribune*, Op Ed Agriculture, Chandigarh, 8 July.

———. 2016. 'Smallholder Organisation through Farmer (Producer) Companies for Modern Markets: Experiences of Sri Lanka and India'. In Jos Bijman, Roldan Muradian, and Jur Schuurman (eds), *Cooperatives, Economic Democratization and Rural Development*, 75–100. Edward Elgar Publishing.

———. 2018. 'Reforming Agricultural Markets in India: A Tale of Two Model Acts'. *Economic and Political Weekly* 53(51): 44–49.

———. 2019. 'Re-organising Agricultural Markets for Doubling Farmer Incomes in India: Relevance, Mechanisms, and Role of Policy'. *Indian Journal of Agricultural Economics* 74(3), July–Sept: 390–407.

three

# Legislating Contract Farming Practice*

## The Model Contract Farming Act, 2018

Contract farming has been growing in importance globally. The Food and Agriculture Organisation of the United Nations (FAO) reported that by the turn of the century (2000), 45 per cent of cash crop and livestock farmers were growing under contract (Chazovachii et al. 2021). Contract farming can be defined as a system for the production and supply of agricultural and horticultural and other allied produce by farmers/primary producers under advance contracts; the essence of such arrangements being a commitment to provide an agricultural commodity of a type (quality/variety) at a specified time, price, and in specified quantity to a known buyer. In fact, CF can be described as a halfway house between independent farm production and corporate/captive farming, and can be considered a step towards complete vertical integration or disintegration depending on the given context. Due to the efficiency (co-ordination and quality control in a vertical system) and equity (smallholder inclusion) benefits of this hybrid system, it has been promoted aggressively

*Most of this chapter was earlier published as part of an article by the author in the *Economic and Political Weekly* titled 'Reforming Agricultural Markets in India: A Tale of Two Model Acts', and has been reproduced here with permission. *See* Singh (2018).

in the developing world by various agencies (Glover 1987). It involves four specifications—pre-agreed price, quality, quantity or acreage (minimum/maximum), and time (Singh 2002). It is generally undertaken when there is market failure expressed in perishability of produce, quality of produce, and technicalities of producing a new/different product (Bijman 2008).

Contract farming is known by different variants like the centralised model, which is the company–farmer arrangement; the outgrower scheme, which is run by government/public sector/joint venture; the nucleus–outgrower scheme, involving both captive farming and CF by the contracting agency; the multi-partite arrangement involving many types of agencies; the intermediary model where agents are involved between the company and the farmer, and satellite farming referring to any of the above models (Bijman 2008; Eaton and Shepherd 2001; GoI 2003). In fact, CF varies depending on the nature and type of contracting agency, technology, nature of crop/produce, and the local and national context (Swain 2011).

The contracts could be of three types: (*i*) procurement contracts under which only sale and purchase conditions are specified; (*ii*) partial contracts wherein only some of the inputs are supplied by the contracting firm and produce is bought at pre-agreed prices; and (*iii*) total contracts under which the contracting firm supplies and manages all the inputs on the farm and the farmer becomes just a supplier of land and labour. The relevance and importance of each type varies from product to product and over time and these types are not mutually exclusive (Bijman 2008; Hill and Ingersent 1987; Key and Runsten 1999). Whereas the first type is generally referred to as marketing contracts, the other two are types of production contracts (Scott 1984; Welsh 1997). But there is a systematic link between product and factor markets under the contract arrangement as contracts require definite quality of produce and therefore, specific inputs (Little and Watts 1994; Scott 1984). Also, different types of production contracts allocate production and market risks between the producer and the processor in different ways. The price of the contracted produce can be growers' fixed price, residual (profit/loss) sharing by sponsor and grower, open market-based price, spot market price, consignment-based price, two-part split price, tournament price (fixed plus variable, based on relative performance), base price plus quality-based incentive price, or administered price.

For different reasons, both farmers and farm product processors/distributors/exporters may prefer contracts to complete vertical integration. A farmer may prefer a contract which can be terminated at reasonably short notice. Also, contracting gives access to additional sources of capital, and a more certain price by shifting part of the risk of adverse price movement to the buyer (Hill and Ingersent 1987). Farmers also get an access to new technology and inputs, including credit, through contracts which otherwise may be outside their reach (Eaton and Shepherd 2001; Glover 1987). For a contracting agency, contracts are more flexible in the face of market uncertainty, make smaller demands on scarce capital resources, and impose less of an additional burden of labour relations, ownership of land, and production activities, on management (Kirk 1987). The firm even gets an access to unpaid family labour (White 1997) and can make use of state funds indirectly through the agricultural production sector, funds which are directed at farmers by development agencies (Clapp 1988). Also, food processors can minimise their overhead costs per unit of production by operating their plants at or near-full capacity as contracting gives assured and stable raw material supplies from farms. The firm can also project an image of working with local producers as a partner when it undertakes CF, and may thus even obtain statal and international agency incentives for its activities which are then seen as developmental projects, instead of corporate farming (Kirk 1987). Contracts also help improve product quality by directly introducing incentives and penalties to counter the problems of adverse selection and moral hazard in any contractual arrangement resulting in under investment or shirking by any of the parties (Wolf et al. 2001).

At a more macroeconomic level, contracting can help to remove market imperfections in produce, capital (credit), land, labour, information, and insurance markets; facilitate better co-ordination of local production activities which often involve initial investment in processing, extension etc.; and can help in reducing transaction costs, including the farmer's (Bijman 2008; Grosh 1994; IFPRI 2005; Key and Runsten 1999). From an institutional economics perspective, the logic for contract farming could also come from the creation of positive externalities like employment, market development or infrastructure, if agribusiness firms create them better than the open market or the state (Key and Runsten 1999). Contract farming figures as an institutional arrangement/innovation for agricultural development (Glover 1987).

Some others recommend contract farming as the only way to make small-scale farming competitive as the services provided by contracting agencies cannot be provided by any other agencies (Eaton and Shepherd 2001). Contract farming is also an alternative to corporate farming which may be costly, risky, and difficult to manage and still not viable (Payer 1980). Further, in India, the factors that encourage the spread of contract farming across crops and regions since they provide new space in this alternative arrangement, more so in the context of increasing withdrawal of the state from agricultural space, are: food supermarket chain growth, including Foreign Direct Investment (FDI) in retail; international trade and quality issues like Sanitary and PhytoSanitary (SPS) measures in organic trade; fair trade and ethical trade; promotion of contract farming by the central and state agencies; banking and input industry push for contract farming; farming crisis and reverse tenancy; and the failure of traditional cooperatives. Even the new Intellectual Property Regime (IPR) which encourages protection and exploitation of proprietary genetics is likely to accelerate contract farming practice (Wolf et al. 2001). Further, under the new agricultural policy regime, public-private partnership is the main route being taken to bring about transformation in agriculture, and the state is providing incentives to corporates to enter the agribusiness sector, including through contract farming. Contract farming is a better co-ordination strategy or option for raw material procurement as it is better than open market (arms-length) transactions and complete vertical integration (captive production). Whereas open market procurement does not meet quality and timing or assured availability concerns of a buyer, complete vertical integration can be costly and difficult to reverse.

Though contract farming is receiving a push from many stakeholders, there are many factors like the APMC regulation in Gujarat and Haryana, improving open market efficiency, Minimum Support Price (MSP) policy, corporate farming including leasing of wastelands, and an overwhelming presence and interest of NGOs in the farming sector, which will act as dampeners to the growth and spread of contract farming. However, corporate farming can also work favourably if corporate agencies resort to leasing of these lands to contract growers, or provide contractual access to these lands to small and marginal farmers and landless labour since corporate farming is unlikely to be viable.

There are different models being practised by different players in the sector which range from bi-partite to multi-partite and intermediary-based (see Appendix for Table 3.1 and Figures 3.1 to 3.7). It is interesting to note that given the diversity of rural and agricultural landscape in India, a single contracting agency

(Frito Lay) practises five different models in different states of India for the same crop (chip grade potatoes). Table 3.1 shows that most of the crops covered under CF are those with some market failure either in terms of farmer involvement or market signals. Most of these are high-value crops which require new and higher investments for producing for the market. Therefore, they need risk coverage—both production risk and market risk, and more of the latter.

## Pricing

The contracting agencies, including those contracting organic produce, and the fresh food retail chains give market price-based prices to their contract or 'contact' farmers (Singh 2009a; Singh and Singla 2011). The question which should be asked is: Is this a fair practice since in India, market prices fluctuate so widely? If market prices were efficient, why did the chains have to go to growers? Most of the liberalisation in the farm sector, including abolition of the APMC Act in Bihar, has been on the basis of the assumption that APMC markets have behaved monopsonistically and therefore, need to be done away with or made to compete with other channels. If that was true, why should a buyer go back to the same mandi to discover its procurement price? This is a serious issue as even a remarkable premium over market price may not help a farmer if open market prices go down significantly, which is not uncommon in perishable produce markets in India. Thus, the issue of what is fair price for the primary grower remains, as there is little transparency in pricing and costing of operations. This kind of practice also compromises the market-risk reduction role of CF.

Globally, there have been issues with the CF practice (Chambers 2015; Chazovachii et al. 2021) like side selling, mistrust, and dissatisfaction among contract growers about company practices, and therefore, unwillingness to continue, or withdrawal from contracts (Ruml and Qaim 2020).

The Model Contract Farming and Services Act, 2018 uses the concept of family farms which is not really relevant in the Indian context because if 86 per cent farms are marginal or small (less than 2 ha.) and have been producing commercially for so many decades, how can they be compared with family farms in the US or Europe, where the proportion of such farms is much smaller though their average farm size is much larger? In fact, the Act cites operational inefficiency of small (calling them 'handkerchief size'!) farms as the reason for promoting contract farming. It is difficult to understand how the scale of farm operation can change due to CF as the only way to achieve some semblance of scale under CF is to have group contracts which, unfortunately, the Act does not even mention. The Act provides for a CF facilitation group at village/ panchayat level to facilitate contract arrangement and its delivery for the two parties. It is surprising that it could think of this group, but not of the much-needed group contracts. Such group contracts are already in practice in Gujarat in crops like potato.

In fact, group contract is the most desirable provision in the Indian context and in any smallholder context, as there is provision for group certification under GLOBALG.A.P. as well as for organic and fair trade, and there are many exporters in India in crops like basmati rice, grapes, and baby corn, who work with groups of farmers for group certification but have individual contracts with each farmer. That is where group contract farming had a role to play. Even Thailand, which has much larger average landholding size than India, formally mandated the group contracts as a part of its four-sector cooperation plan for agricultural development, where contract farming was the central mechanism, and the state's extension and low-cost credit were two important components of the four-sector plan along with private contracting agencies and farmer groups (Singh 2005a).

Further, it is stated that crop insurance is to be a part of CF arrangement which is much needed to reduce farmer's production risk in the absence of any other mechanism, especially when high-value crops are much more prone to risk. Even price- or market-linked insurance provided by any public agency would be applicable to the contracted produce. Even multi-partite agreements are allowed under the Act, which is the name of the game increasingly as individual agencies cannot afford to provide all services and take risk of default. These are good aspects of the Act.

The Act also introduces a new service contract which refers to the:

> agreement between the farmers/FPO and services contract sponsor wherein [the] former supplies the produce and the latter provides post-harvest management and marketing services to the produce like storage, primary value addition and such other services in the food value chain including marketing linkage to organised retailers, processors, exporters, future/option trading etc. (MoAFW 2018: 6).

This is completely irrelevant in this Act as service provision can be a part of the CF arrangement itself. Perhaps the agro-input companies and other professional service agencies are being referred to here which undertake contract farming for other buyers, and not for their own needs. This has been the practice in India across many crops and states where agro-input companies have organised contract farming projects for processors and exporters under the previously amended APMC Acts (Singh 2009a). There was no need to separate out this set of players as they also undertake contract farming activity like any other player.

## Regulation versus Facilitation

Like the APLMA, 2017, the APLCFSA, 2018 also bids goodbye to regulation as an objective as it is titled the APLCFS (*Promotion and Facilitation*) Act (emphasis added). In fact, this Model Act does not even have the Model CF agreement which was a part of the 2003 Model Act. The 2003 Model Act had mandatory and optional provisions of the CF agreement specified in the Act and the mandatory ones were an essential part of the model contract agreement (APMC Model Act, 2003). This again suggests that it is left to the parties to the contract to decide on all aspects of the agreement, even when global and local agencies are already looking at responsible contract farming agreements (FAO and IISD 2018). On the other hand, the Act goes on to state that the sponsor shall have to make all arrangements for purchase and provide materials required for filling and weighing/measuring of the produce in advance when the produce is to be taken by the producer for delivery to the sponsor at the agreed place (MoAFW 2018: 30). When all other terms and conditions have been left for the two parties to mutually agree on, why these were mandated is not clear since the place and time of delivery and all the arrangements related to it are essential aspects of any contract farming agreement, besides price, acreage or quantity of produce, and quality parameters. Similarly, the payment schedule is also specified by the Act in terms of payment through electronic clearance, which is two-third of the value of bought produce to be paid at the time of delivery itself and the rest after assessment of quality. If assessment of quality is pending, how can the buyer pay for the produce?

That the committee has gone overboard in facilitating contract farming for the benefit of private agencies as against farmers' interest is also clear in the fact that the Act has provision for the producer leasing out agricultural land to the sponsor-leasee for contract farming under this Act, which is not inconsistent with state's law or any other law in force at present (MoAFW 2018: 26). The question arises: How can a committee mandated to legislate on contract farming step into the domain of land-leasing issues when there is a separate model Land Leasing Act proposed by the NITIAayog and when there are state-level laws to permit or restrict land leases? This clearly would allow sponsors full access to farmland, not just through contract farming, and encourage corporate farming disguised as contract farming.

In fact, for the first time, under the Model Act, CF (Promotion and Facilitation) Board is seen as a guide and an umpire, which would popularise crops under contract farming in domestic and export markets as a brand. It is difficult to see how a regulatory body can engage in promotion of this mechanism when its primary role should be conflict resolution and monitoring of contract farming projects. This is especially surprising as the title of the Act does not even mention regulation. In fact, it is stated that the CFS (Contract Farming and Services) Board would also promote Farmer Producer Organisations (FPOs) including Producer Companies (PCs) and would frame quality/grade standards. In fact, it is even mentioned that the Board may also represent in the meetings/workshops of farmers and FPOs organised by a sponsor to facilitate them to understand the contracts under this Act, the relevant law, and other things incidental thereto. This is what the shift from regulation to facilitation means! Surely these are not desirable functions/powers of a regulatory agency—Why should a state-funded body promote markets for private agencies, especially when they are supposed to explore their own markets and invest in them? Once a regulatory body becomes a part of the activities of the party (contract farming sponsor) it is supposed to regulate, there is a potential conflict of interest.

## Antithesis of CF

The Act also exempts a CF buyer from any APLM fee by default—this was provided for in the previous Model Act (2003) as well but the new Act creates a new CFS Board fund with 0.3 per cent of the value of contracted produce charged as facilitation fee from CF sponsor, which is capped at 0.5 per cent of the value of the contracted produce, besides grants and sums it receives from other sources. This fee can also be waived initially to promote contract farming as an incentive. This is bringing back market fee in another form though the argument was that the CF agencies need not pay the market fee as they do not use mandi facilities. So, is this fee to be paid because the Board would promote contract-farmed produce for the sponsors in domestic and export markets?

More surprising is the provision which states that the Board would ensure buying of entire pre-agreed produce of grower by the contracting agency, which goes against the very logic of quality promotion and standards in the market. Though it sounds good to protect producer interest this way, but it would be quite problematic to ensure this, because when a contract specifies quality standards beforehand, why should a buyer buy lower quality produce which the buyer may not need? In practice, contracting agencies do buy some of the lower quality produce as part of the agreement to give a market outlet for the farmers, but it is always a source of conflict as the prices offered for this rejected or lower quality produce (sometimes on flimsy grounds) are very low or nominal (Singh 2008).

More surprisingly, the Act links contract price to market price which is the antithesis of contract farming philosophy. The driving factor behind undertaking contract farming is that the desired quality of produce at reasonable cost are not available to the agency in the open market. Since the new Act compels the agency to go by market prices which may not be efficiently discovered, the question arises as to why the agency should go for contract farming at all. In fact, one of the states in India (Haryana) under the 2003 Model Act, had linked the contract price to the MSP of whichever crop it was relevant for, and that was seen as an undesirable step as contract price cannot be tied to any other price mandatorily, as the costs and yields can also be grounds for farmers to get into contract farming, and not just price.

The Act has so many inadequacies that it does not seem to have provided for the diversity of the agricultural sector in India. For example, CF sponsor can be a person, but what about FPOs? Surprisingly, the FPOs/FPCs are given the status of only a producer which can contract with sponsors on behalf of the producers, and not as contracting agencies which could also offer contracts to their members and non-members. Why cannot they also undertake contract farming with members and even non-members? This again shows that out-of-the-box and innovative mechanisms have been ignored. In fact, one way to make FPOs/FPCs more vibrant business entities is to bring contractual relations with their members in a value chain-driven world so that they can attend to markets more competitively with reliable supplies and can contain opportunistic behaviour of their members. In fact, while buying agencies like processors, exporters, or supermarkets help create new value, it is FPOs which help capture a part of the value so created, for their members (Gersch 2018).

The above discussion of the various provisions of the draft APLCFS Act shows that the Act was meant to open up the agricultural markets without adequate safeguards for farmers who are the primary stakeholders of the system. The very exclusion of the alternate channels from the APLMC domain also shows that the reforms are stuck in the middle due to their political economy dimensions, and the inability and unwillingness of the state governments to bell the cat in most cases, and this only reflects escapism from the reality of mainstream agricultural markets in India. The various lacunae of the Act show that it was prepared in a hurry without much discussion and debate and would not serve the purpose of making contract farming more efficient and inclusive, which is the need of the times and when it is possible to include small producers in value chains profitably (Singh 2016b). That is rather unfortunate as contract farming is a much-needed vehicle to bring new crops, technologies, and markets to farmers.

## References

Bijman, J. 2008. 'Contract Farming in Developing Countries: An Overview', Working paper. Development Co-operation, Ministry of Foreign Affairs, and Wageningen University, The Netherlands.

Chambers, A. 2015. 'Building Enabling Environment for Contract Farming Success', USAID Policy Brief No. 6, February. USAID.

Chazovachii, B., C. Mawere, and L. Chitongo. 2021. 'Sustainability of Centralized Contract Farming among Tobacco Smallholder Farmers in Makoni North District, Zimbabwe'. *Cogent Social Sciences* 7: 1–14.

Clapp, R. A. J. 1988. 'Representing Reciprocity, Reproducing Domination: Ideology and the Labour Process in Latin American Contract Farming'. *The Journal of Peasant Studies* 16(1): 5–39.

Eaton, C., and A. W. Shepherd. 2001. 'Contract Farming: Partnerships for Growth'. Rome: Food and Agriculture Organization of the United Nations.

FAO. 2012. *Guiding Principles for Responsible Contract Farming Operations*. Rome: FAO.

FAO and IISD. 2018. *Model Agreement for Responsible Contract Farming, With Commentary*. Rome: FAO.

FICCI (Federation of Indian Chambers of Commerce & Industry). 2012. 'Corporate Interventions in Indian Agriculture', September, PPT presentation.

Gersch, I. 2018. 'Producer Organisations and Contract Farming: A Comparative Study of Smallholders' Market Strategies in South India'. *Zeitschrift für Wirtschaftsgeographie* 62(1): 14–29.

Glover, D. 1987. 'Increasing the Benefits to Smallholders from Contract Farming: Problems for Farmers' Organisations and Policy Makers'. *World Development* 15(4): 441–448.

Grosh, B. 1994. 'Contract Farming in Africa: An Application of the New Institutional Economics'. *Journal of African Economies* 3(2), October: 231–261.

GoI (Government of India). 2003. *Contract Farming Agreement and its Model Specifications*, 17 September. New Delhi: Ministry of Agriculture, Department of Agriculture and Co-operation, Krishi Bhawan.

GoR (Government of Rajasthan). 2020. *The Farmers (Empowerment and Protection) Agreement on Price Assurance and Farm Services (Rajasthan Amendment) Bill, 2020*, Bill No. 31 of 2020. Govt. of Rajasthan.

Hill, B. E., and K. A. Ingersent.1987. *An Economic Analysis of Agriculture*. London: Heinemann.

IFPRI (International Food Policy Research Institute). 2005. 'High Value Agriculture and Vertical Co-ordination in India—Will the Smallholders Participate?' Draft research report. Washington: IFPRI.

Kalamkar, S. S. 2012. 'Inputs and Services Delivery System under Contract Farming: A Case of Broiler Farming'. *Agricultural Economics Research Review* 25: 515–521.

Kaur, P., and N. Singla. 2018. 'Can Contract Farming Double Farmers' Income?' *Economic and Political Weekly* 53(51): 68–73.

Key, N., and D. Runsten. 1999. 'Contract Farming, Smallholders, and Rural Development in Latin America: The Organisation of Agroprocessing Firms and Scale of Outgrower Production'. *World Development* 27(2): 381–401.

Kirk, C. 1987. 'Contracting Out: Plantations, Smallholders and Transnational Enterprise'. *IDS Bulletin* 18(2): 45–51.

Kumar, P. 2006. 'Contract Farming through Agribusiness Firms and State Corporation: A Case Study in Punjab'. *Economic and Political Weekly* 41(52): 5367–75.

Lambrecht, I. B., and C. Ragasa. 2018. 'Do Development Projects Crowd-out Private Sector Activities? Evidence from Contract Farming Participation in Northern Ghana'. *Food Policy* 74: 9–22.

Little, P. D., and M. J. Watts (eds). 1994. *Living Under Contract—Contract Farming and Agrarian Transformation in Sub-Saharan Africa*. Madison: University of Wisconsin Press.

Mayers, J., and S. Vermeulen. 2002. *Company–Community Forestry Partnerships—From Raw Deals to Mutual Gains?* London: International Institute for Environment and Development (IIED).

Melese, A. T. 2012. 'Contract Farming: Business Models that Maximise the Inclusion of and Benefits for Smallholder Farmers in the Value Chain'. *Uniform Law Review* 17(1–2): 291–306.

Minten, B., L. Randrianarison, and J. F. M. Swinnen. 2006. 'Global Supply Chains, Poverty and the Environment: Evidence from Madagascar'. In J. F. M. Swinnen (ed.), *Global Supply Chains, Standards and the Poor*, CAB International, 147–158.

MoAFW. 2018. *Model Act [The State/UT Agricultural Produce and Livestock Contract Farming and Services (Promotion and Facilitation) Act, 2018]*, February. MoAFW, Department of Agriculture, Co-operation and Farmers' Welfare, Government of India.

———. 2020. *The Farmers (Empowerment and Protection) Agreement on Price Assurance and Farm Services Bill*, No. 11 of 2020.

———. 2020. *The Farmers (Empowerment and Protection) Agreement on Price Assurance and Farm Services Bill*, No. 11 of 2020-Guidelines for Farming Agreement.

Opondo, M. 2000. 'The Socio-economic and Ecological Impacts of the Agro-industrial Food Chain on the Rural Economy in Kenya'. *Ambio* 29(1): 35–41.

Pande, S. 2008. 'Firm on the Farm', *Business Today* 19(16), 8 August: 46–48.

Payer, C. 1980. 'The World Bank and the Small Farmer'. *Monthly Review* 32(6): 30–46.

Pritchard, B., and J. Connell. 2011. 'Contract Farming and the Remaking of Agrarian Landscapes: Insights from South India's Chilly Belt'. *Singapore Journal of Tropical Geography* 32(3): 236–252.

Ragasa, C., I. Lambrecht, and D. S. Kufoalor. 2018. 'Limitations of Contract Farming as a Pro-Poor Strategy: The Case of Maize Outgrower Scheme in Upper West Ghana'. *World Development* 102: 30–56.

Ray N., G. Clarke, and P. Waley. 2021. 'The impact of contract farming on the welfare and livelihoods of farmers: A village case study from West Bengal'. *Journal of Rural Studies* 86: 127–135.

Rickson, R. E., and D. Burch. 1996. 'Globalised Agriculture and Agri-food Restructuring in Southeast Asia: The Thai Experience'. In D. Burch, R. E. Rickson, and G. Lawrence (eds), *Globalisation and Agri-Food Restructuring—Perspectives from the Australasia Region,* 323–344. Brookfield (USA): Avebury.

Ruml, A., and M. Qaim. 2020. 'Smallholder Farmers' Dissatisfaction with Contract Schemes in Spite of Economic Benefits: Issues of Mistrust and Lack of Transparency'. *The Journal of Development Studies* 57(7).

Sako, M. 1992. *Prices, Quality and Trust—Inter-Firm Relations in Britain and Japan*. Cambridge: CUP.

Schupbach, J. M. 2014. 'Foreign Direct Investment in Agriculture—The Impact of Outgrower Scheme and Large-Scale Farm Employment on Economic Wellbeing in Zambia', PhD thesis. University of Zurich.

Scott, C. D. 1984. 'Transnational Corporations and Asymmetries in the Latin American Food System'. *Bulletin of Latin American Research* 3(1): 63–80.

Sharma, N. 2016a. 'Determining Growers' Participation in Contract Farming in Punjab'. *Economic and Political Weekly* 51(2): 58–65.

______. 2016b. 'Does Contract Farming Improve Farmers' Income and Efficiency? A Case Study from Punjab'. *Economic and Political Weekly* 51(40): 63–69.

Sharma, N., and S. P. Singh. 2015. 'Exploring Contract Relationships in Punjab: A Case Study of Potato and Basmati Paddy'. *Journal of Land and Rural Studies* 3(2): 165–186.

Shrimali, R. 2014. 'Spaces of Corporate Control in Agriculture: A Critical Study of Contract Farming in the Indian State of Punjab', PhD thesis. Toronto: York University.

Singh, G., and S. R. Asokan. 2005. *Contract Farming in India—Text and Cases*. New Delhi: Oxford & IBH.

Singh, M., J. Singh, and S. Kumar. 2015. 'Comparative Economics of Contract and Non-contract Farming of Barley in Punjab'. *Journal of Agricultural Development and Policy* 25(2): 46–56.

Singh, M. P. 2007. 'Contract Farming and Emerging Agrarian Structure: The Case of Punjab', Unpublished PhD thesis. New Delhi: Jawaharlal Nehru University.

Singh, R., K. Anuj, S. Satyavir, and C. Ramesh. 2013. 'Prospects and Problems of Malt Barley Cultivation through Contract Farming in Rajasthan'. *Journal of Global Communication* 6(1): 1–6.

Singh, S. 2000a. 'Co-operative as Contractor: A Case Study of Contract Farming by a Co-operative Marketing Federation in the Indian Punjab'. *Co-operative Perspective* 35(2).

———. 2000b. 'Theory and Practice of Contract Farming – A Review'. *Journal of Social and Economic Development* 2(2), July–December.

———. 2002. 'Contracting Out Solutions: Political Economy of Contract Farming in the Indian Punjab'. *World Development* 30(9): 1621–1638.

———. 2003. 'Contract Farming in India: Impacts on Women and Child Workers', IIED Gatekeeper Series No.111. London: International Institute for Environment and Development.

———. 2004. 'Crisis and Diversification in Punjab Agriculture: Role of State and Agribusiness'. *Economic and Political Weekly* 39(52): 5583–5590.

———. 2005a. 'Role of the State in Contract Farming in Thailand: Experience and Lessons'. *ASEAN Economic Bulletin* 22(2): 217–228. (*ASEAN Economic Bulletin* renamed as *Journal of Southeast Asian Economies* from 2013).

———. 2005b. *Political Economy of Contract Farming in India*. New Delhi: Allied Publishers.

———. 2005c. 'Changing Structure and Organisation of Agriculture and Small Farmers in India'. *Social Change* 35: 1–31.

———. 2008. 'Marketing Channels and their Implications for Smallholder Farmers in India'. In E. B. McCullough, P. L. Pingali, and K. G. Stamoulis (eds), *The Transformation of Agri-food Systems: Globalization, Supply Chains, and Smallholder Farmers*, 279–310. Rome: FAO, and London: Earthscan Press.

Singh, S. 2009a. *Organic Produce Supply Chains in India: Organization and Governance*. New Delhi: Allied Publishers.

______. 2009b. 'Supply Chains for High Value Crops: A Case Study of Mint in Punjab'. *Indian Journal of Agricultural Marketing* 23(1): 93–102.

______. 2010. 'Globalisation and Sustainability Issues in Agriculture in Asia—A Case of India'. In S. Gill, L. Singh, and R. Marwah (eds), *Economic and Environmental Sustainability of the Asian Region*, 23–44. New Delhi: Routledge.

______. 2011. 'Contract Farming for Sustainable Agricultural Development in India: A Smallholder Perspective', IGIDR Proceedings of Workshop on 'Policy Options and Investment Priorities for Accelerating Agricultural Productivity and Development in India', 10–11 November, held at IIC, New Delhi.

______. 2012. *Modern Food Value Chains in India: Emerging Potential for the Poor.* New Delhi: Samskriti.

______. 2013a. 'The Practice of Contract Farming in India: Making it Inclusive and Effective'. *Food Chain* 3(3): 137–154.

______. 2013b. 'Regulating Contract Farming—Punjab Way', *The Tribune*, Op. Ed. Agriculture, Chandigarh, 8 July.

______. 2016a. 'Smallholder Organisation through Farmer (Producer) Companies for Modern Markets: Experiences of Sri Lanka and India'. In Jos Bijman, Roldan Muradian, and Jur Schuurman (eds), *Cooperatives, Economic Democratization and Rural Development*, 75–100. Edward Elgar Publications.

______. 2016b. 'Inclusive Food Value Chains in India: Evidence and Drivers'. In C. Ramasamy and K. R. Ashok (eds), *Vicissitudes of Indian Agriculture in a Growing Economy: Challenges, Strategies and the Way Forward.* New Delhi and Mumbai: Academic Foundation and Indian Society of Agricultural Economics.

______. 2018. 'Reforming Agricultural Markets in India: A Tale of Two Model Acts'. *Economic and Political Weekly* 53(51): 44–49.

______. 2020a. 'Tale of Two Flawed Agri Ordinances', *The Hindu Business Line*, Opinion, 21 June.

______. 2020b. 'Farm Laws: Design Leaves Much to Be Desired'. *Ideas for India*, 13 October.

Singh, S. 2020c. 'Farmers' Freedom at Stake', *Frontline*, 23 October, 27–31.

———. 2021. *Understanding Performance and Impact of Producer Companies: Case Studies across States and Promoters in India*. Final report, March. Ahmedabad: CMA, IIM.

Singh, S., and N. Singla. 2011. *Fresh Food Retail Chains in India: Organisation and Impacts*. New Delhi: Allied Publishers.

Singh, S., and T. Singh. 2014. *Producer Companies in India: Organisation and Performance*. New Delhi: Allied Publishers.

Swain, B. B. 2011. 'Contract Farming in Andhra Pradesh: A Case of Rice Seed and Gherkin Cultivation'. *Economic and Political Weekly* 46(42): 60–68.

Vaswani, L. K., V. Venkatakrishnan, R. Upadhay, and J. Talati. 2003. *Agriculture-Market Linkages: Evaluating and Evolving a Conceptual Framework in Indian Context*. NABARD Occasional Paper No. 28. Mumbai: NABARD.

Welsh, R. 1997. 'Vertical Co-ordination, Producer Response, and the Locus of Control over Agricultural Production Decisions'. *Rural Sociology* 62(4): 491–507.

White, B. 1997. 'Agro-industry and Contract Farming in Upland Java'. *The Journal of Peasant Studies* 24(3): 100–136.

Wolf, S., B. Hueth, and E. Ligon. 2001. 'Policing Mechanisms in Agricultural Contracts'. *Rural Sociology* 66(3): 359–381.

# Appendix to Chapter 3

**Figure 3.1: Bi-partite CF model**

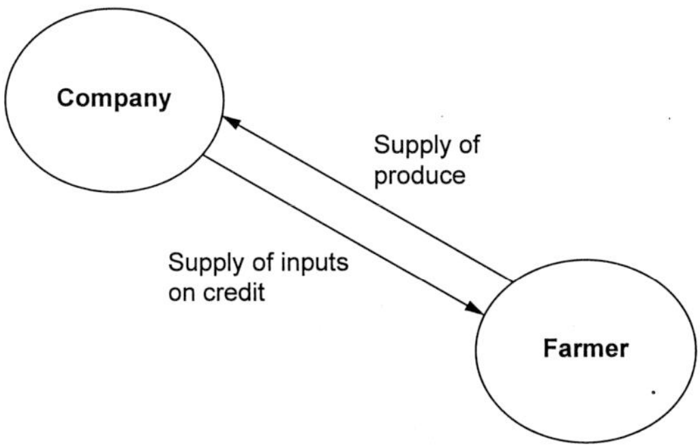


*Source*: Singh (2004).

**Figure 3.2: Tri-partite CF model**

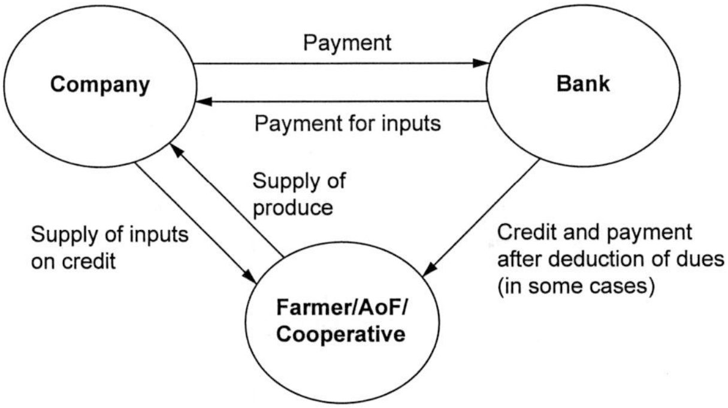


*Note*: AoF stands for Association of Farmers.
*Source*: Singh (2005c).

**Figure 3.3: State-led contract farming system in Punjab (original model)**

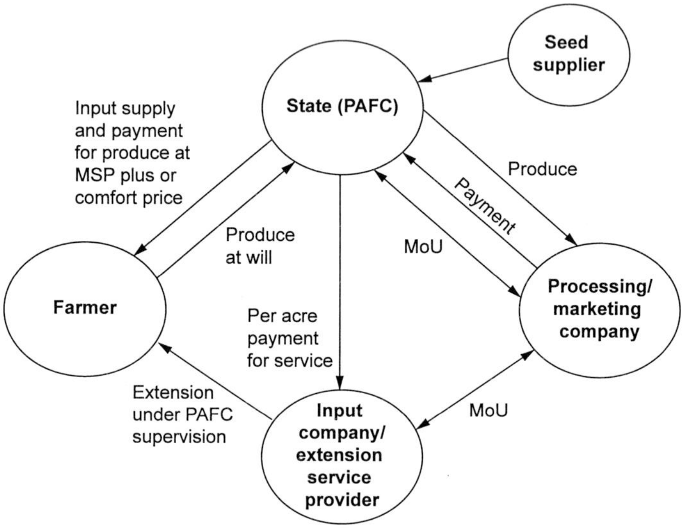


*Source*: Singh (2004).

**Figure 3.4: State-led contract farming system in Punjab (revised model)**

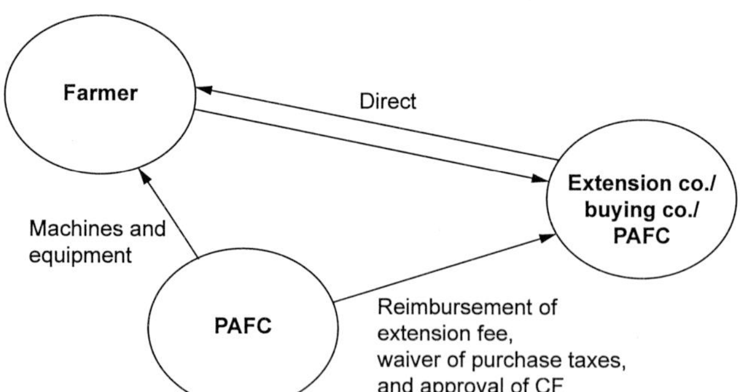


*Source*: Singh (2005c).

**Figure 3.5: Quad-partite CF model**

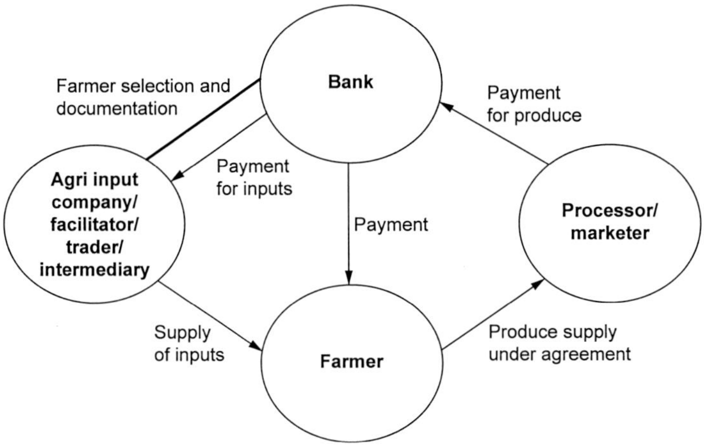


*Source*: Singh (2004).

**Figure 3.6: Six-partite (networking) CF model**

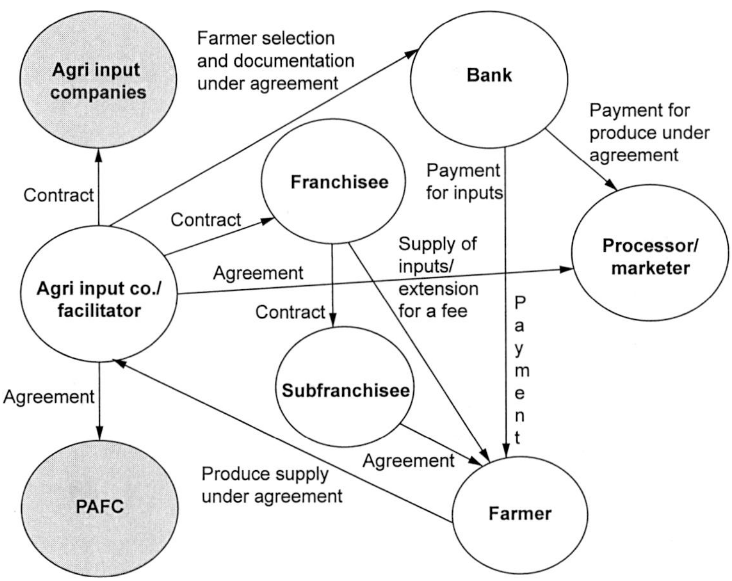


*Source*: Singh (2005c).

**Figure 3.7: Tri-partite (intermediary) model of CF**

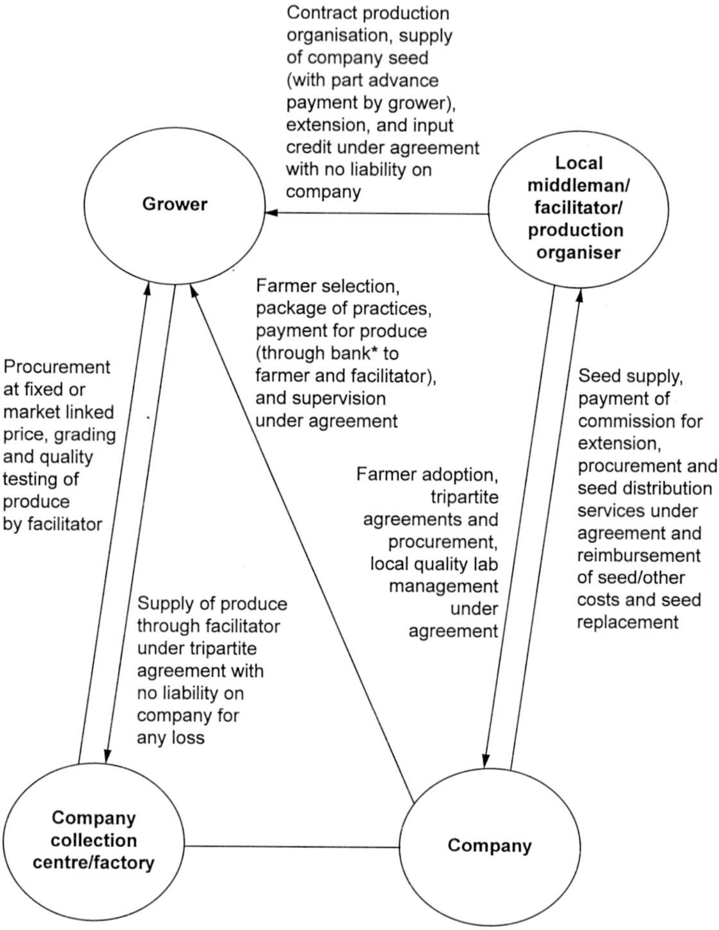


*Notes*: *Bank finances contract production at Rs 10,000/acre (NABARD norm is Rs 13,000/acre for the given crop) at 7.5 per cent rate of interest. It receives the money from the company for payment to the farmer for his produce, from which it pays the facilitator (as per authorisation given by the grower), deducts its own dues, and transfers the remaining amount in the farmer's bank account.

*Source*: Singh (2005c).

**Table 3.1: Crop- and company-wise spread of contract farming in India**

| *Company* | *Location* | *Type of linkage* | *Crop/product* | *Farmers (no.) and acreage (acres)* | *Average area under contract (acres)* |
|---|---|---|---|---|---|
| UB Group | Punjab, Rajasthan | Through Pepsi | Barley | 1,300 farmers, 10,000 acres | 8 |
| SAB Miller | Rajasthan | CF | Barley | 8,150 farmers | |
| Field Fresh Foods | Punjab, Maharashtra | Direct CF and through franchisees | Baby corn and sweet corn | 1,000 farmers, 4,000 acres | 4 |
| Global Green | Karnataka, Andhra Pradesh, and Tamil Nadu | CF | Gherkin | 25,000 farmers in 2012 (31,000 in 2008) (10,00 + 4000 + 11000) 15,857 acres | 0.64 |
| Intergarden | Karnataka | CF | Gherkin | 4,460 farmers (as of 2004) | |
| Vishal | Karnataka | CF | Gherkin | 600 farmers | |
| Namdhari Fresh | Karnataka | CF | Vegetables | 1,200 farmers, 4,800 acres | 4 |
| TN Project | Tamil Nadu | CF | Guar (cluster bean) | 80 acres | |
| Safal (NDDB) | UK/UP | CF through associations | Vegetables | 150 associations, 18,000 farmers | |
| AVT McCormick | Karnataka and AP | CF | Chilli | 430 farmers, 2,125 acres | 5 |
| DFV (P&PAG) | Gujarat, Maharashtra | CF | Banana | 2,150 farmers, 8,600 acres | 4 |
| Sanghar Exports | Maharashtra | CF (for Bahraini Group N&E) | Banana | 100 farmers, 400 acres | 4 |

*(Contd)*

*Table 3.1 (Contd)*

| *Company* | *Location* | *Type of linkage* | *Crop/product* | *Farmers (no.) and acreage (acres)* | *Average area under contract (acres)* |
|---|---|---|---|---|---|
| Jain Irrigation | Maharashtra | CF | White onion | 1,800 farmers, 4,200 acres | 2.3 |
| Pepsi | Punjab/ Haryana/ Maharashtra/ Jharkhand/ Karnataka/ West Bengal/ Gujarat | CF: direct/ indirect | Potato | 12,000 farmers (6,500 in WB alone), 16,000 acres (2,600 acres in WB alone) | 1.33 |
| McCains Foods India | Gujarat | CF | Potato | 750 farmers | |
| Siddhivinayak Agri | Maharashtra | CF through franchisees | Potato | 1,000 farmers, 1,500 acres | 1.5 |
| MSSL | Maharashtra | CF | Grapes | 400 farmers, 2,000 acres | 5 |
| Nandan Biomatrix | AP and three more states | CF through franchisees | Jatropha | 40,000 acres | |
| Trikaya Foods | Maharashtra | CF | Patchouli/ lettuce | | |
| Deepak Fertilizers | Maharashtra | CF | Grapes/ pomegranate/ onion/banana | 2,000 farmers | |
| Tina Oils and Chemicals | Maharashtra | CF | Soyabean and sunflower | 60,000 farmers, 2,36,000 acres | 4 |
| Biotor (formerly Jayant) | Maharashtra, Gujarat, Punjab | CF | Castor | 25,000 farmers, 1,00,000 acres (65,000 in MH alone) | 4 |
| Shakti Soya | Tamil Nadu | CF: indirect | Soyabean | | |
| C & M Group, Nasik | Maharashtra | CF | Soyabean and maize | 2,200 farmers | |

*(Contd)*

*Table 3.1 (Contd)*

| *Company* | *Location* | *Type of linkage* | *Crop/product* | *Farmers (no.) and acreage (acres)* | *Average area under contract (acres)* |
|---|---|---|---|---|---|
| HUL | Gujarat | CF: direct | Chicory | 1,700 farmers, 4,500 acres | 2.5 |
| L&T | Chhattisgarh | CF | Safed musli | | |
| Herbs India | Kerala | CF | Safed musli, Stevia | | |
| AM Todd | Punjab/UP/ UK/Haryana | CF | Mint | 2,000 farmers, 10,000 acres | 5 |
| Dabur | West Bengal | CF | Pineapple | | |
| Nadukuda Pvt Ltd | Kerala | CF | Pineapple | | |
| Garlico Industries | MP | CF | Garlic and white onion | | |
| Sami Labs | Karnataka | CF | Med. plants | | |
| Sunstar Organics | Haryana | CF | Organic Basmati | 280 farmers, 1,200 acres | 4.3 |
| Satnam Overseas | Haryana/ Punjab | CF | Basmati | | |
| Agrocel | Gujarat/ Haryana | CF | Organic Basmati/ cotton/ sesame | 2,200 farmers, 3,500 acres | 1.6 |
| UOCB | Uttarakhand | CF | Organic Basmati | 440 farmers, 500 acres | 1.1 |
| HAFED | Haryana | CF | Basmati | | |
| Markfed | Punjab | CF | Basmati | | |
| LT Overseas | Punjab/ Haryana | CF through Pepsi | Basmati | 4,000 farmers, 10,000 acres | 2.5 |
| Pepsi | Punjab | CF | Basmati | 300 farmers, 2,000 acres | 6.67 |
| Satluj Agri | Punjab/ Haryana/ Uttar Pradesh | CF | Organic Basmati | 50 farmers, 2,200 acres | 44 |
| Rallis | Uttar Pradesh | CF | Wheat | 19,000 acres (as of 2003) | |

*(Contd)*

*Table 3.1 (Contd)*

| *Company* | *Location* | *Type of linkage* | *Crop/product* | *Farmers (no.) and acreage (acres)* | *Average area under contract (acres)* |
|---|---|---|---|---|---|
| TCL | North India | CF-informal | Basmati | 45,000 acres | |
| Adat Farmers' Co-op. Bank | Trissur | CF for Nest Group, Cochin | Paddy, rice | 2,300 farmers, 250 acres | 0.1 |
| Suminter India Organics | Across north India | CF | Organic produce | 13,000 farmers, 71,000 acres | 5.5 |
| Sresta Natural Bioproducts (24 Letter Mantra) | Across India, mainly AP, Maharashtra | CF: direct and through NGOs | Organic produce | 5,000 farmers, 10,000 acres | 2 |
| Ion Exchange Farms | Maharashtra | CF | Organic fruits: cashew, mango | | |
| Maikal BioRe | MP | CF | Organic cotton | 1,700 farmers, 12,885 acres | 7.6 |
| Amit Green Acres | Gujarat | CF | Organic cotton and sesame | 500 farmers, 3,200 acres | 6.4 |
| Eco Farms | Maharashtra | CF | Organic cotton | 7,000 farmers, 50,000 acres | 7.1 |
| Mahima | MP | CF | Organic produce | 600 farmers, 10,000 acres | 16.7 |
| Pratibha Syntax | MP | CF | Organic cotton | 2,700 farmers, 22,000 acres | 8.1 |
| NCC Shri Cotton, Akola | Maharashtra | CF | Cotton | 1,684 farmers, 16,818 acres | 10 |
| Virchandnarsingh Cotton | Maharashtra | CF | Cotton | 1,551 farmers, 4,632 acres | 3 |
| Mohta Spinning | Maharashtra | CF | Cotton | 1,294 farmers, 3,717 acres | 30 |
| Shri NCC Santosh Fibres | Maharashtra | CF | Cotton | 3,720 farmers, 18,785 acres | 5 |
| Super Spinning | Tamil Nadu | CF | Cotton | | |
| Apachi Cotton | Tamil Nadu | CF | Cotton | | |

*(Contd)*

*Table 3.1 (Contd)*

| *Company* | *Location* | *Type of linkage* | *Crop/product* | *Farmers (no.) and acreage (acres)* | *Average area under contract (acres)* |
|---|---|---|---|---|---|
| INHERE | Uttarakhand | CF | Organic produce | 2,269 farmers (350 SHGs), 1,000 acres | 0.44 |
| Morarka Foundation | All India | CF | Organic produce | | |
| Himalaya Healthcare | Karnataka | CF | Ashwagandha | 1,750 acres | |
| Dhawan Intl | Uttarakhand | Direct | Med. plants | | |
| Dabur India | AP | CF | Amla (Indian gooseberry) | 1,042 acres | |
| HUL | Gujarat | CF | Chicory | | |
| Seed companies (35–40) | All over India including NSC/SSCs | CF: direct and through organisers | Seed | Each one with a few hundred farmers for each crop and a few hundred acres | |
| Palm oil (Godrej, Palm Tech, SICAL, Radhika) | AP | CF: direct | Palm | 95,000 acres | |
| Cauvery Oil Palm | Tamil Nadu | CF: direct | Palm | 209 farmers, 4,375 acres | 21 |
| Suguna Poultry and Hatcheries | Tamil Nadu | CF | Chicken | 15,000 farmers across, 8,000 villages and 11 states | |
| Venkateshwara Hatcheries | MH/AP/TN | CF | Chicken | | |
| Swathi Hatcheries | Tamil Nadu | CF | Chicken | Of the total broiler production, 37 per cent is under contract farming and 78 per cent is from south India | |

*(Contd)*

*Table 3.1 (Contd)*

| *Company* | *Location* | *Type of linkage* | *Crop/product* | *Farmers (no.) and acreage (acres)* | *Average area under contract (acres)* |
|---|---|---|---|---|---|
| Arambagh Hatcheries | West Bengal | CF | Chicken | | |
| Patel Farms | Gujarat | CF | Emu | 35 farmers | |
| Champion Agro | Rajkot, Gujarat | CF | Baby corn | 2,500 acres | |

*Note*: CF stands for contract farming.

*Source*: FICCI 2012; Kalamkar 2012; Pande 2008; Pritchard and Connell 2011; Singh 2009a; Singh and Asokan 2005; Singh and Singla 2011; Vaswani et al. 2003; websites of the companies mentioned and data from field studies by the author.

four

# The Farmers' Produce Trade and Commerce (Promotion and Facilitation) Act, 2020[*]

## Inadequate Rationale and Implications

### Introduction

In 2020, the Union Ministry of Agriculture and Farmer Welfare (MoAFW) framed two new Acts (repealed in 2021) on agricultural produce wholesale markets and contract farming (besides amending the Essential Commodities Act, 1955), as mentioned earlier, to allow and encourage new market channels in terms of buying from, or working directly with farmers. These were parallel to state governments modifying their APMC Acts, following the Model APMC Acts suggested by the Union MoAFW. The new Union Acts on agricultural markets (constitutionally, a state domain) intended to achieve a unified national market; provide choice to farmers when selling their produce, with better price discovery; and attract private investment in agricultural markets. Instead, the Acts attracted serious opposition from farmer unions and many political parties despite the government claiming and

[*]A shorter version of this chapter was first published as an online article by The Hindu Centre for Politics and Public Policy in March 2021, and has been reproduced here in a revised form with their kind permission. See Singh (2021).

highlighting various benefits of the new Acts. To recapitulate what we touched upon in Chapter 1, seven state governments (Punjab, Rajasthan, Chhattisgarh, Delhi, Kerala, Tamil Nadu, and West Bengal) passed resolutions against these Acts in their legislatures, and three states also attempted to amend the Union Acts at their levels to enhance protection of the interests of farmers and other stakeholders.

The Congress Party-ruled states planned to nullify the three central laws on agricultural markets and provide for alternatives of their own for protection of farmer interest, especially on prices for their produce. This was executed in three states—Punjab, Chhattisgarh, and Rajasthan, which passed amendments to the central Acts in their assemblies. Punjab took the lead but ended up focusing on paddy and wheat prices by making MSP as the minimum purchase price for any buyer in any channel and penalising any violation of that; besides the state government aiming to protect its own revenue. Chhattisgarh acquired the power for the state government to declare or set up any place as 'deemed' mandi, including private wholesale markets for regulation of notified agricultural produce, and empowered the market committee or the State Agricultural Marketing Board (SAMB) to order production of accounts of any buyer regarding purchase and sale of the notified agricultural produce from any person, and also inspect godowns and vehicles and seize them. But it did not make MSP mandatory for any purchase unlike Punjab or Rajasthan.

Rajasthan amended the Farmers' Produce Trade and Commerce (Promotion and Facilitation) Act, 2020 to restore what it called 'the safeguards for the farmers of the state' as under the state's APMC Act. It aimed to bring back the status quo by restoring the domain of the state APMC Act as it was before 5 June 2020 (when the Farm Laws were promulgated as ordinances). However, unlike

Punjab's MSP provision for two crops, the Rajasthan amendment, like Chhattisgarh's, steered clear of the MSP issue and only made the 'harassment' of the farmer by any buyer a punishable offence with not less than three years and upto seven years of imprisonment, or fine upto not less than Rs 5,00,000, or both. The harassment of the farmer was defined as:

> where the trader does not accept the delivery of the farm produce agreed upon or having accepted the delivery does not make the payment to the farmer in accordance with the terms of the agreement or within three days from the date of receipt of delivery of good whichever is earlier (GoR 2020).

For this offence, all the directors or partners of the company were to be held guilty if they were serving the company at the time of commitment of such offence.

But like the Punjab provision of punishment for the compulsion or exertion of pressure on the farmer to sell the produce at below MSP, the Rajasthan provision of 'harassment of the farmer' would have been very difficult to establish on the ground. Also, could the state government afford to buy at MSP if the private players refused to offer such a price and move to other states, given that central government procurement in Rajasthan was not very high, unlike in Punjab?

In this context, this chapter discusses major aspects of the Farmers' Produce Trade and Commerce (Promotion and Facilitation) Act, 2020 (FPTC Act). The next section examines the major contents of the FPTC Act, assesses the goodness of its rationale, and places the spotlight on the realities behind the fears and perceptions surrounding its implications for farmers, commission agents, and APMC mandis. The concluding section discusses ways forward from a farmer-interest protection perspective.

## The Farmer's Produce Trade and Commerce Act, 2020

The FPTC Act intended to promote efficient, transparent, and barrier-free inter-state and intra-state trade of farm produce outside the physical premises of markets or deemed markets notified under various state agricultural produce marketing legislations. It also sought to create a facilitative framework for electronic trading. However, as its intent was to bypass the existing (APMC) mandi system, it is also referred to as the 'Mandi bypass Act' (Narayanan 2020).

Previously and as of now again (after the repeal of the new Farm Acts of 2020), under the state APMC Acts, there was a notified market area from which all produce was to be transacted within the designated APMC yards and sub-yards, or else buyers had to seek permission under the amended APMC Acts as per the Model APMC Act, 2003 and Model Agricultural Produce and Livestock Marketing (Promotion and Facilitation) Act, 2017 (APLMA). The permission had to come from the local APMC, for buying outside the mandi or undertaking contract farming. However, the produce could still be subject to the same or similar taxes and levies as the produce transacted inside the market yard.

It was important to note that the rationale for the 2020 reforms is based on the assumption that the majority or most of the farm produce passed through APMC mandis, and that these mandis had not been discovering prices efficiently, and not letting other channels like direct purchase, private wholesale markets, and contract farming flourish as there was a conflict of interest involved. But the reality is that only 17–25 per cent produce goes through APMC mandis. This is also due to the fact that there are far fewer mandis than needed (only 7,000 against 42,000 needed), and as per the recommendation of the National Commission for Farmers, a mandi should be available to a farmer within a radius of

5 kms (Narayanan 2020; Shah 2021). Further, in major agricultural states, APMCs are multi-stakeholder elected bodies. Only Punjab has not had an election to APMCs in the last 40 years.

The new Act created a new 'trade area' outside the APMC market yards, where any buyer with a Permanent Account Number (or PAN, which is an income tax ID in India) could buy directly from farmer sellers, and the state government could not have imposed any taxes on such a transaction. Hence, the new central Act would lead to the creation of two parallel markets in each mandi town instead of a single market. Also, in September 2020, the Haryana government tried to stop neighbouring Uttar Pradesh farmers from selling paddy at MSP in Haryana, which shows that inter-state barriers were not so easy to remove by central regulation, unless states are on board for such opening up of markets (*NDTV* 2020). Similarly, the Food Corporation of India (FCI) buying from APMC mandis in Punjab through the arthiyas, even after the new Act came into effect, sent a message contrary to the spirit of the Act (Singh 2020a).

More significantly, the Act included trader-to-trader transactions within a state or across states under the definition of farmer produce. How can this be justified since once the primary transaction is completed, it stops being farmer produce as farmer is no longer involved in this transaction? This is similar to the Farmer Producer Organisations (FPOs) asking for exemption from income tax on their income, arguing that since they deal with their member farmers' produce who are exempted from paying income tax, FPOs should also be exempted from income tax (Singh 2020a).

Importantly, the 'new trade area' had no provision for counterparty risk coverage, unlike the APMC system where all buyers and facilitators are licensed by the APMC and have to pay licensee fees and bank guarantees, so that farmer risk against any payment default could be secured.

Further, some of the provisions, such as payment to farmer by trader on the same day, or within a maximum of three days if procedurally so required, were worse than what already existed under the APMC Act in some states. For example, in Madhya Pradesh, payment for the produce bought in the market yard has to be paid on the same day to the seller, right at the market yard (MPSAMB 2005).

The hope that this kind of opening up of markets would have brought new investments in agriculture were also misplaced, if one went by the experience of states like Kerala which never had an APMC Act; or Bihar, which repealed the APMC Act in 2006 (Bera 2021; Singh 2015); or Maharashtra, which delisted fruits and vegetables from APMC in 2018. It is important to note that laws cannot substitute for policy. Therefore, a policy has to be in place to develop the agricultural sector as a whole. New investment would need incentives, and not just ease of doing business (Singh 2020b).

That the Indian state felt that the APMC Acts which were brought in to protect farmer interest from the traders and commission agents had become outdated, and saw them as restrictive and monopsonistic, and sought space for private sector participation (as if traders in APMCs are not private), reflected the changing perspective of the state on agricultural markets from regulation to promotion and facilitation of the private corporate sector (Shrimali 2021).

In the FPTC Act, 2020, a 'trader' meant a person who bought farmers' produce by way of inter-state trade or intra-state trade or a combination thereof, either for self or on behalf of one or more persons for the purpose of wholesale trade, retail, end-use, value addition, processing, manufacturing, export, consumption or for such other purpose, and included a retail consumer! This kind of definition which includes even retail consumers was never used to define agricultural trade or traders as it was always and should always be defined in terms of parties involved in wholesale transaction, including first-level transaction which was between farmers and first-buying trader.

The Madhya Pradesh APMC Act defines a trader as 'a person who in his normal course of business buys or sells any notified agricultural produce and includes a person engaged in processing of agricultural produce but does not include an agriculturalist as defined in clause (b) of this subsection'.

So far as the role of FPOs in value chains or farm produce markets is concerned, the FPTC Act provided for e-markets by FPOs although one was not sure how many of them could make use of this opportunity, given their poor capital and professional resources. This was similar to APMCs allowing private wholesale markets by such collectives and many such markets already exist in Maharashtra.

In what could have been adverse to FPOs, they were treated as farmers under the Union Act. Section 2-b of the FPTC Act stated: '"farmer" means an individual engaged in the production of farmers' produce by self or by hired labour or otherwise and *includes the farmer producer organisation*' (emphasis added; MoAFW 2020). This is despite the fact that FPOs are not involved in production as most of them carry out pre- and post-production operations such as aggregation, trading, and value addition.

At the same time, the trading role of the FPO was explicit in Section 4-1 which stated:

> Any trader may engage in the inter-State trade or intra-State trade of scheduled farmers' produce with a farmer or another trader in a trade area:
>
> Provided that no trader, except the farmer producer organisations or agricultural co-operative society, shall trade in any scheduled farmers' produce unless such a trader has a permanent account

number allotted under the Income-tax Act, 1961 or such other document as may be notified by the Central Government.

This duality could create problems. Moreover, FPOs were not explicitly named as a part of the definition of person on the buying side, while cooperatives and cooperative societies were. There was even a separate payment mechanism proposed and rules provided for FPOs. It was not clear why this was needed and why producer members' own agencies like Amul need to be told by government when and how to pay their members.

## Inadequate Rationale for New Trade and Commerce Act

Besides the fact that the timing of the new laws itself became indefensible for various reasons, there were other issues with the need for new laws. It was argued and believed by most lay people interested in the issue of Farm Laws and many experts that APMC markets had become monopsonistic (a market characterised by a single buyer) due to collusion among traders in these markets, which did not discover prices efficiently and suffered from poor modern infrastructure. Therefore, it was reasoned that farmers needed to be given a choice of channels and better price discovering markets like private wholesale markets, e-markets, or new trade areas where farmers and buyers could just negotiate a price mutually.

Burman et al. (2018) examined the rationale for enabling a national market for food. They argue that the Constitution of India obligates the Union government to achieve a national market for food. They point out the rigidities and restrictions in the agricultural market structure especially the APMC Act, 2003 which they argue promoted local monopsonies. It is argued that the reforms in the APMC system have failed to remove restrictions in the inter-state trading of agricultural products. In fact, they argue that the very existence of APMCs creates barriers to trade in agricultural goods and in the development of a functional market. They cite the example of the Karnataka APMC Act wherein the private wholesale markets are discouraged from coming into existence as the Act requires a minimum distance between an APMC and a private wholesale market. They argue that when for most other commodities there are no restrictions on buyers and sellers, why not have similar freedom of transactions even in agricultural goods? They propose that such a competitive local market in food commodities can be created by the Union government using its powers under the constitution which could override the existing restrictive framework in place in most states. They cite Article 301 of the Constitution of India, which states that trade and commerce throughout India shall be free with only reasonable restrictions, which legislatures at the Union and the state level can impose in public interest. They argue that APMC Acts are nothing but such restrictions which come under this power to impose restrictions. They opine that legal sanctions placed by the states on trade in agricultural goods and technical barriers to trade, like border checks between states and tax compliances, prevent a national market in food from happening.

Burman et al. (2018) also point to the role of state governments in enforcing the Essential Commodities Act, restricted future markets, and arbitrary export and import controls as additional barriers to a national market. The argument for removing these constraints is that this will increase local competition by bringing in more private players and facilitate intra-state and inter-state trade, which is what a national market for food is about. Though they appreciate the delisting of fruits and vegetables from the APMC Acts in many states beginning with Maharashtra in 2012 and Bihar repealing the APMC Act in 2006; these are termed as only an incremental reform and not good enough to remove the legally mandated monopsonies and restrictions. List 1 of the Seventh Schedule is cited to argue that the parliament has legislative power to regulate all inter-state trade and commerce and also regulate intra-state trade and commerce, and the production, supply, and distribution of food stuffs including edible oilseeds and oil. They agree that Entry 14 of the State List in the Seventh Schedule gives the state legislature executive authority over agriculture but argue that when there is a specific constitutional requirement for a national market, this power does not hold. They argue that parliamentary action on creating a national market would trump state laws if Article 301, Entry 33 of List 3 (Concurrent List), Entry 26 of List 2 and Entry 42 of List 1 of the Constitution of India are read together. They cite a legal judgment to make this argument wherein Bihar lost the case against a sugar company which was asked to pay the market fee under the state APMC Act as sugar was already under a separate Sugarcane Act, but the court restricted the application of APMC Act only to supply and distribution of goods as well as trade and commerce within the market and market areas, even though agriculture, agricultural markets, and fairs were under the State List of subjects. However, this example does not seem very relevant here because, as the authors note, this was about the legal supremacy of two state Acts between themselves.

Burman et al. (2018) cite another Supreme Court case between the State of Assam and a tea company wherein the Supreme Court held that Article 301 applied not only to inter-state trade, commerce, and intercourse but also to intra-state trade, commerce, and intercourse. This way Article 301 was seen as imposing a limitation on the constitutional powers of the parliament and state legislature. Hence, they argue that any laws (Union or state) which impede free trade and commerce has to be invalid under Part 13 even if they are otherwise valid in their enactment. Based on the above analysis, Burman et al. propose that a national market in food can be created by using the powers under the Union and the Concurrent List to replace existing framework on agricultural marketing with a modern framework. They suggest using Part 13 and 33 of List 3 of the Seventh Schedule to draft a law which allows farmers and traders of agricultural commodities absolute freedom to buy and sell across states, and overrides state APMC laws which would make APMC markets just one among a number of market channels which come up in a competitive market for farmers to sell in. They even go further and suggest that this would still not achieve the purpose of removing monopolistic practices in food storage, distribution, and marketing and therefore, suggest using Article 307 of the Constitution to create a statutory body to review laws and regulations creating procedures that restrict the free movement of the food products (ibid.).

Before this, the Economic Survey of 2014–15 had also proposed this kind of approach though a bit cautiously:

> There are provisions/entries in List III of the Seventh Schedule (Concurrent List) in the Constitution which can be used by the Union to enact legislation for setting up a national common market for specified agricultural commodities...Once a law is passed by the Parliament to regulate trading in the specified agricultural commodities, it will override the state APMC laws, paving the way for creating a national common market. But this approach could be seen as heavy-handed on the part of the Centre and contrary to the new spirit of co-operative federalism (as quoted in Kumar 2022).

Further, despite all the claims being made in popular debates about the consultations held and repeated pleas made by various committees and commissions for APMC reforms, it is a fact that none of the committees ever recommended enactment of a common law by the Union of India, or argued for creation of a 'new trade area' outside the APMC under the control of the Union of India (Kumar 2022).

Chand (2020) argues that the new Farm Acts have been widely acclaimed at home and abroad as historical and long overdue. He argues that the narrative has been created based on ideological and imaginary grounds to build opinion and pressure against the new laws by ignoring the intent, content, and implications of the new policy reforms. He cites 10 major reasons as the rationale for introducing such reforms in the agricultural sector which include: the growing disparity between farm/agricultural and non-farm/agricultural income; growing imbalance between domestic demand and supply of various food commodities; need for improving export competitiveness of Indian agriculture; the robust growth of high-value crops without MSP support indicating liberalised markets being more favourable for agricultural growth than government support and intervention in market; need for local market access for smallholders who have small volumes of produce; integration of fragmented markets; need for desired raw materials for the growth of food processing; growing inter-state movement of agricultural commodities due to specialisation and commercialisation of agriculture supporting one nation–one market; need for higher private sector investment in the farm sector; and need for reducing the fiscal burden of MSP-based procurement on the government. He also argues that these reforms are not sudden and have been attempted at the Union-government level since the Model APMC Act in 2003, including deregulation of fruits and vegetables during the United Progressive Alliance (UPA) regime in many states; he laments that when the states did not come on board to reform their APMC Acts for 18 long years, the only option with the Union government was to use the constitutional route. He recognises that more than half of the marketable surplus is sold outside the APMC mandis but still uses this information to provide a rationale for the Farmers' Produce Trade and Commerce Act (FPTC Act), 2020.

Chand believes that 'if reforms are encouraged in the right direction by the states, it won't take long for farmer producers or their FPOs to become price dictators rather than remaining price takers' (2020: 8). He also believes that the FPTC Act would have resulted in compressing the value chains and eliminating excessive intermediation. He is of the view that after 2006, no growth in mandi (APMC) infrastructure happened, and APMC markets became a revenue generation activity for state governments and a rent-seeking avenue for many other stakeholders under the cover of regulation. He notes that buying charges for wheat and paddy in Punjab and Haryana which are mostly bought by FCI are four to six times higher than that for Basmati rice purchased by private buyers. He is of the view that the states which have higher buying charges should lower these to 1.5 per cent which would make APMCs compete with the private markets. He is also clear in stating that the MSP is being unnecessarily linked with new Acts as MSP and procurement are purely administrative decisions, and some states like Bihar and Kerala have been procuring at MSP without having APMC structure or regulation. He cites the case of the Maharashtra APMC Act amendment of 2018 and the Fair and Remunerative Price (FRP) for sugarcane, which did not go well as a legal or mandatory price for farm produce by the private buyers, and this model cannot be sustainable. He even makes an argument that in Bihar, after the scrapping of the APMC Act, the farm harvest prices which were 30 per cent below MSP 10 years before the repeal, went down to 20 per cent during the decade after the repeal, although the FPTC Act did not abolish the APMC mandi system unlike the Bihar repeal of the APMC Act. He believes that the new Acts would have benefitted when APMC mandis and the private market coexisted and competed.

He concludes 'if they are implemented in the right spirit, they will take Indian agriculture to the new heights and usher in the transformation of the rural economy' (ibid.: 19).

However, the comparisons with high-value crops like milk and sugarcane also miss the point that there are strong cooperative institutions in these sectors which protect farmer interest through competitive pricing and other means even though there is no MSP in these crops.

But, it is important to note that as per NSS–SAS 2013 data (Gopikuttam and Naik 2020), APMC mandis accounted for only between 25–63 per cent of the first disposal of crops by farmers, compared with 28–71 per cent going through private trade, 3–20 per cent across crops through the input dealers, and 0–19 per cent through cooperatives and other government agencies. There were also significant state-level variations across crops for channel used by farmers; for example, in the case of rice in Punjab, mandis accounted for 59 per cent of first disposal compared with only 17 per cent in Bengal, whereas across the states of Uttar Pradesh, Punjab, and Madhya Pradesh, APMC mandis accounted for more than 40 per cent of the first disposal, and government agencies, accounted for 34 per cent and 39 per cent of the first disposal in Madhya Pradesh and Punjab, respectively.

In terms of crop-wise implementation of MSP-based procurement, it varied from 0.5 per cent in gram and soyabean to 3 per cent in cotton and more than 30 per cent in rice and wheat in 2017–18 (Gopikuttam and Naik 2020). Even in wheat and paddy, government agencies procured less than one-third of total production over the years (Table 4.1). Here again, there were very high state-level variations with almost no procurement of paddy in Uttarakhand in 2017–18 to as high as 31 per cent in Punjab and 11 per cent in Andhra Pradesh and Haryana. Similarly for wheat, Punjab accounted for 38 per cent of the total procurement followed by Haryana at 28 per cent while Rajasthan had 4 per cent share in the total. In case of plantation crops like areca nut and pepper in Karnataka, 100 per cent of the procurement in the APMC was by the cooperative societies and these cooperatives gained profits and paid significant incentives to their members. The cooperatives ended up buying 50 per cent of areca nut and 32 per cent of pepper in 2019–20 (ibid.).

**Table 4.1: Procurement of wheat and paddy as against their production (in million tonne)**

| *Year* | *Production of wheat* | *Procurement of wheat for central pool by government agencies* | *Production of rice* | *Procurement of rice for central pool by government agencies* |
|---|---|---|---|---|
| 2002–03 | 65.76 | 19.02 | 71.82 | 16.42 |
| 2003–04 | 72.15 | 15.80 | 88.53 | 22.88 |
| 2004–05 | 68.64 | 16.79 | 83.13 | 24.68 |
| 2005–06 | 69.35 | 14.78 | 91.79 | 27.65 |
| 2006–07 | 75.81 | 9.22 | 93.35 | 25.10 |
| 2007–08 | 78.57 | 11.12 | 96.69 | 28.73 |
| 2008–09 | 80.68 | 22.68 | 99.18 | 34.10 |
| 2009–10 | 80.8 | 25.38 | 89.09 | 32.03 |
| 2010–11 | 86.87 | 22.51 | 95.98 | 34.19 |
| 2011–12 | 94.88 | 28.33 | 105.3 | 35.04 |
| 2012–13 | 93.51 | 38.14 | 105.24 | 34.04 |
| 2013–14 | 95.85 | 25.09 | 106.65 | 31.84 |
| 2014–15 | 86.53 | 28.02 | 105.48 | 32.04 |
| 2015–16 | 93.5 | 28.08 | 104.32 | 34.21 |
| 2016–17 | 98.51 | 22.96 | 109.69 | 38.10 |
| 2017–18 | 98.61 | 30.82 | 111.51 | 36.48* |
| **Total** | **1340.02** | **358.74** | **1557.75** | **487.53** |

*Note*: *Figures as on 6 July 2018.

*Source*: LSS (2019).

**Table 4.2: Who sells where: Crop and channel/agency-wise sales (in percentage) by sample farmers**

| *Channel →*<br>*Crop ↓* | *Local market**<br>*(% of total sales)* | *APMC* | *Government agency* | *Co-op* | *FPO* | *Private processor* | *CF agency* | *Others* | *Total* |
|---|---|---|---|---|---|---|---|---|---|
| Paddy | 70–75<br>(62) | 1.7–3.2<br>(2.7–8.4) | 7.3–13.3<br>(13.9–18.4) | 3.4–5.4<br>(3.6–7.8) | 0–0.1<br>(0–0.1) | 3.6–5.7<br>(2.7–8) | 0.4–0.5<br>(0.7–1) | 2.5–3<br>(0.6–1.2) | 100 |
| Arhar | 65.4–76<br>(68–78) | 12.4–24.6<br>(18.7–22.1) | 1.2–1.7<br>(1.3–1.7) | 0–0.2<br>(0–0.1) | 1.2–1.7<br>(0–0.3) | 1–4.3<br>(0.9–6.8) | 0<br>(0) | 3.9–6.7<br>(0.5) | 100 |
| Sugarcane | 15.6–25.3<br>(12.6–15.8) | 1.3–2.2<br>(2.7–3.4) | 10.1–15.2<br>(6.8–15.9) | 14.1–20.7<br>(16.7–25.3) | 0<br>(0) | 29.4–37.6<br>(27–33.8) | 3.4–5.7<br>(7–12.1) | 6.8–10.7<br>(5.2–13.1) | 100 |
| Groundnut | 73.5<br>(54.7) | 11.9<br>(18.6) | 1.1<br>(0.6) | 0.6 | 0<br>(0) | 6.9<br>(11.8) | 0<br>(0) | 4.5<br>(12.1) | 100 |
| Cotton | 59.5–71.8<br>(53.6–69) | 8.9–13.9<br>(9.7–19.7) | 2.4–10.6<br>(0.1–2.3) | 0.3–1.1<br>(0.4–0.6) | 0–0.1<br>(0.1) | 6.4–8.8<br>(5.2–9.9) | 0–0.1<br>(0–0.2) | 1.3–1.4<br>(1.4–1.8) | 100 |
| Soyabean | 70.6<br>(63.1) | 19.6<br>(21.6) | 3.4<br>(6.7) | 0.6<br>(1.0) | 0<br>(0) | 4.8<br>(7) | 0<br>(0.1) | 0.1<br>(0) | 100 |
| Coconut | 88.1<br>(78.8–83.6) | 1.6<br>(3–4.5) | 0.1<br>(0) | 0.3<br>(0.1–0.4) | 0<br>(0.1) | 1.3<br>(1.5–1.7) | 0<br>(0) | 6.9–7.2<br>(1.4–1.8) | 100 |
| Jowar | 75.3–86.5<br>(80.7–92.7) | 4.3–11.5<br>(2.7–7.1) | 0.7–1.9<br>(0.7–3.3) | 0.4–0.9<br>(0.4–1.7) | 0<br>(0) | 1.9–4.4<br>(0.6–3.9) | 0.1–0.2<br>(0.1–0.2) | 2.5–3.7<br>(1.6–2.7) | 100 |
| Maize | 87.5–88.9<br>(83.3–89.8) | 1.2–5<br>(2.7–6.7) | 1–1.9<br>(1.6–2) | 0.3–0.6<br>(0.1–1.4) | 0<br>(0.1) | 1.9–3.3<br>(1.6–3.2) | 0<br>(0) | 1.1–4.2<br>(0.3–1.2) | 100 |
| Wheat | 81<br>(66.1) | 5.7<br>(12.7) | 4<br>(13.5) | 1.8<br>(3.3) | 0<br>(0) | 2.5<br>(1.6) | 0<br>(0) | 4.1<br>(1.5) | 100 |

*(Contd)*

*Table 4.2 (Contd)*

| *Channel →* <br> *Crop ↓* | *Local market** <br> *(% of total sales)* | *APMC* | *Government agency* | *Co-op* | *FPO* | *Private processor* | *CF agency* | *Others* | *Total* |
|---|---|---|---|---|---|---|---|---|---|
| Gram | 79.7 <br> (70.1) | 9.2 <br> (15.1) | 1.9 <br> (3.1) | 1.5 <br> (3.8) | 0.1 <br> (0.1) | 3.1 <br> (5.1) | 0 <br> (0) | 3.7 <br> (1.8) | 100 |
| Moong | 82.9–87.4 <br> (76.4–92.9) | 7.1–8.5 <br> (4.5–19.1) | 0.3–1.4 <br> (0.3–1.3) | 0–0.4 <br> (0–0.4) | 0 <br> (0) | 0.5–0.7 <br> (0.1–0.3) | 0 <br> (0) | 1.4–6 <br> (0.1–2.1) | 100 |
| Potato | 90–93.2 <br> (81.8–89.8) | 1.7–3.5 <br> (3–7.5) | 0–0.1 <br> (0–0.6) | 0 <br> (0) | 0 <br> (0) | 3.6–4.6 <br> (4.2–6) | 0 <br> (0) | 0.1–2.4 <br> (0.1–4.8) | 100 |
| Onion | 86.4 <br> (87.5) | 5.8 <br> (5.2) | 0 <br> (0) | 0.2 <br> (0) | 0 <br> (0) | 2.1 <br> (1.5) | 0 <br> (0) | 5.1 <br> (5.2) | 100 |

*Notes*: Data for 2018–19; *figures in parentheses are % sold in each channel of the total output sold. The range for some crops is as they were sold in both Kharif and Rabi seasons in the same region or across different regions of India.

*Source*: Based on NSO (2021).

Even 2018–19 data from NSO shows that APMC mandis and government agencies accounted for only a small percentage of total sales of different crops by farmers (Table 4.2). Even in potato and tomato in Punjab, only 32 per cent farmers sold in wholesale markets and 42 per cent did not sell any produce at all in wholesale markets. Farm gate sales and processors accounted for 11 per cent and 30 per cent respectively, of potato and tomato sales of farmers (Singh, G. 2020). Further, though the SC Committee report has been criticised for not being methodologically sound or even representative of farmers in its stakeholder surveys (Shylendra 2022), it also finds that 57.7 per cent of the farmers and farmer groups it surveyed reported selling outside the APMC mandis (SC Committee 2021), which reconfirms the fact that APMC mandis are not monopsonistic and dominant players in India's agricultural markets. Its own data analysis also shows that APMC markets did not account for more than 30 per cent of total arrivals across various types of farm produce, and procurement of paddy, wheat, cotton, oilseeds, or pulses through these markets was not even more than 10 per cent of the total value of agricultural produce (SC Committee 2021).

## The Farmers' Produce Trade and Commerce Act, 2020: Issues and Implications

First, it is questionable if the agricultural produce directly sold by farmers can be described as 'trade and commerce' as they do not engage in trade and commerce, as also claimed by farmer unions. Therefore, one can argue that agricultural marketing cannot be legislated as a trade and commerce activity, which will bring it under the ambit of Entry 33 of the Concurrent List, paving the way for Union legislation. To support this point, transactions between an APMC-licensed trader and another APMC or outside trader who buys from this trader are anyway not under the purview of APMCs, as the APMC Act deals only with farmer-level sale of produce: the first transaction between farmer and buyer directly, or through a commission agent and not subsequent transactions (Singh 2020a). Therefore, much ambiguity would have been avoided and farmers' apprehensions not raised if such subsequent transactions, which qualify under 'trade and commerce', had been separately legislated upon under the Union List where Entry 42 has inter-state trade and commerce as its scope.

The view that APMC markets are *sarkari* or are not democratic in most states was not true as vibrant elections are held in major states like Gujarat, Maharashtra, and Karnataka. That APMCs are not government bodies is clear from the recent statement in the Gujarat Assembly where it was stated that Gujarat has 227 cooperative APMCs and 30 private APMCs and only two new private markets had come up during the last two years. Only some states like Punjab have not conducted elections for APMCs for decades and all office bearers have been nominated.

On the issue of infrastructure, a Report (LSS 2019) by the Lok Sabha Standing Committee on Agriculture (2018–2019) pointed out that even as early as 2015, 83 per cent of APMC markets had godown facilities, 66 per cent had covered platforms, 76 per cent had drinking water facilities, and 65 per cent had toilet facilities (Table 4.3). Citing the same survey conducted by the Directorate of Marketing Inspection, the Report pointed out that 38 per cent of these markets had farmer rest houses, 15 per cent even had cold storages, 29 per cent had drying platforms, and 22 per cent had grading facilities (ibid.).

Another argument for bringing in the central Acts was that the states were not reforming markets fast enough and adequately.

**Table 4.3: Infrastructure facilities at APMC mandis in 2015**

| *Facility* | *Percentage of APMCs with said facility* |
|---|---|
| Godown facility | 83 |
| Cold storage | 15 |
| Covered platform | 66 |
| Grading facility | 22 |
| Drying platform | 29 |
| Weighing facility | 49 |
| Drinking water | 76 |
| Toilet | 65 |
| Farmer rest house | 38 |
| Canteen | 32 |
| Banking facility | 7 |
| Internet café | 12 |

*Source*: LSS 2019.

Evidence from the same Standing Committee Report, however, speaks to the contrary (Table 4.4). Even before the Union government's ordinances in 2020, the states had started to implement the Model Acts, which indicates the extent and speed of reforms. By June 2018, a total of 23 states had permitted direct purchase from farmers, 21 allowed e-trading, 23 had single-point levy of market fee, and 22 issued single trading licence for the entire state. In addition, 22 states/UTs had allowed private wholesale markets, 20 permitted contract farming, and 15 even freed fruits and vegetables from APMC regulation altogether (LSS 2019).

To add to the irony, just when the ordinances were brought in during the middle of 2020, 27 out of India's 28 states, and two UTs had already implemented most of the provisions: single licence, single-point levy of market fee, direct marketing, and private wholesale markets, through amendments to their APMC Acts (Table 4.5).

**Table 4.4: Status of adoption of marketing reforms as on 18 June 2018**

| *S.no.* | *Area of reforms* | *Name of the states/UTs which have adopted reforms* |
|---|---|---|
| 1. | Establishment of private market | Andhra Pradesh, Arunachal Pradesh, Assam, Chhattisgarh, Gujarat, Goa, Himachal Pradesh, Karnataka, Maharashtra, Mizoram, Nagaland, Odisha, Rajasthan, Sikkim, Telangana, Tripura, Punjab, UT of Chandigarh, Jharkhand, Uttarakhand, West Bengal, and Uttar Pradesh. |
| 2. | Direct wholesale purchase of agricultural produce from agriculturists (Direct marketing) | Andhra Pradesh, Arunachal Pradesh, Assam, Chhattisgarh, Gujarat, Goa, Haryana, Himachal Pradesh, Karnataka, Madhya Pradesh, Maharashtra, Mizoram, Nagaland, Rajasthan, Sikkim, Telangana, Tripura, Punjab, UT of Chandigarh, Jharkhand, Uttarakhand, Uttar Pradesh, and West Bengal. |
| 3. | Establishment of farmer–consumer market in private sector | Arunachal Pradesh, Assam, Chhattisgarh, Gujarat, Goa, Himachal Pradesh, Karnataka, Maharashtra, Mizoram, Nagaland, Rajasthan, Sikkim, Tripura, Jharkhand, Uttarakhand, Uttar Pradesh, and West Bengal. |
| 4. | Contract farming | Andhra Pradesh, Assam, Chhattisgarh, Goa, Gujarat, Haryana, Himachal Pradesh, Jharkhand, Karnataka, Maharashtra, Madhya Pradesh, Mizoram, Nagaland, Odisha, Punjab (separate Act), Rajasthan, Sikkim, Telangana, Tripura, and Uttarakhand. |
| 5. | Provision for e-trading | Andhra Pradesh, Arunachal Pradesh, Chhattisgarh, Gujarat, Jharkhand, Haryana, Himachal Pradesh, Karnataka, Rajasthan, Sikkim, Goa, Madhya Pradesh, Maharashtra, Mizoram, Telangana, Uttarakhand, Uttar Pradesh, Chandigarh, Tamil Nadu, Punjab, and Odisha. |
| 6. | Single-point levy of market fee across the state/UT | Andhra Pradesh, Arunachal Pradesh, Rajasthan, Gujarat (the value chain players who can get this facility of single-point levy of market fee in Gujarat are processor, grader, packer, value addition, and exporter), Goa, Haryana, Himachal Pradesh, Chhattisgarh, Karnataka, Madhya Pradesh, Maharashtra, Nagaland, Jharkhand, Sikkim, UT of Chandigarh, Punjab, Mizoram, Telangana, Uttar Pradesh, Uttarakhand, Tamil Nadu, West Bengal, and Odisha. |
| 7. | Unified single trading licence for state/UT | Andhra Pradesh, Arunachal Pradesh, Goa, Gujarat, Haryana, Himachal Pradesh, Karnataka, Rajasthan, Chhattisgarh, West Bengal, Madhya Pradesh, Maharashtra, Jharkhand, Mizoram, Nagaland, Telangana, Sikkim, Uttar Pradesh, Tamil Nadu, Uttarakhand, Punjab, and Odisha. |
| 8. | Deregulation of marketing of fruits and vegetables | Madhya Pradesh, NCT of Delhi, Haryana, Assam, Odisha, Gujarat, Himachal Pradesh, Maharashtra, Karnataka, Nagaland, Arunachal Pradesh, West Bengal, Rajasthan, Meghalaya, and Chhattisgarh. |

*Note*: States have made this change in varied legal forms and impacts.

*Source*: LSS (2019).

**Table 4.5: State-wise status of agricultural marketing reforms in India in 2020**

| *S. no.* | *State/UT* | *Limiting regulation within APMC yard* | *Separation of powers between Dir (Mktg) and MD, Mandi Board* | *Single unified trading licence* | *Single-point levy of market fee* | *Private wholesale market* | *Direct marketing (outside mandi)* | *Declaring warehouse, silos / cold storages as deemed market* | *e-trading* | *Deregulation of marketing of fruits and vegetables* |
|---|---|---|---|---|---|---|---|---|---|---|
| 1 | Andhra Pradesh | X | X | ✓ | ✓ | ✓ | ✓ | ✓ | ✓ | ✓ |
| 2 | Arunachal Pradesh | ✓ | ✓ | ✓ | ✓ | ✓ | ✓ | ✓ | ✓ | ✓ |
| 3 | Assam | ✓ | ✓ | ✓ | ✓ | ✓ | ✓ | ✓ | ✓ | ✓ |
| 4 | Bihar | No APMC Act | | | | | | | | |
| 5 | Chhattisgarh | X | ✓ | ✓ | ✓ | ✓ | ✓ | X | ✓ | ✓ |
| 6 | Goa | ✓ | ✓ | ✓ | ✓ | ✓ | ✓ | ✓ | ✓ | ✓ |
| 7 | Gujarat | ✓ | ✓ | ✓ | ✓ | ✓ | ✓ | ✓ | ✓ | ✓ |
| 8 | Haryana | X | ✓ | ✓ | ✓ | ✓ | ✓ | ✓ | ✓ | X |
| 9 | Himachal Pradesh | ✓ | ✓ | ✓ | ✓ | ✓ | ✓ | ✓ | ✓ | ✓ |
| 10 | Jharkhand | X | X | ✓ | ✓ | ✓ | ✓ | ✓ | X | ✓ |
| 11 | Karnataka | ✓ | ✓ | ✓ | ✓ | ✓ | ✓ | ✓ | ✓ | ✓ |
| 12 | Kerala | No APMC Act | | | | | | | | |
| 13 | Madhya Pradesh | X | ✓ | ✓ | ✓ | ✓ | ✓ | X | ✓ | ✓ |
| 14 | Maharashtra | X | ✓ | ✓ | ✓ | ✓ | ✓ | X | ✓ | ✓ |

*(Contd)*

*Table 4.5 (Contd)*

| S. no. | State/UT | *Limiting regulation within APMC yard* | *Separation of powers between Dir (Mktg) and MD, Mandi Board* | *Single unified trading licence* | *Single-point levy of market fee* | *Private wholesale market* | *Direct marketing (outside mandi)* | *Declaring warehouse, silos / cold storages as deemed market* | *e-trading* | *Deregulation of marketing of fruits and vegetables* |
|---|---|---|---|---|---|---|---|---|---|---|
| 15 | Manipur | | | | | No APMC Act | | | | |
| 16 | Meghalaya | ✓ | ✓ | ✓ | ✓ | ✓ | ✓ | ✓ | ✓ | ✓ |
| 17 | Mizoram | X | X | ✓ | ✓ | ✓ | ✓ | X | ✓ | X |
| 18 | Nagaland | ✓ | X | ✓ | ✓ | ✓ | ✓ | ✓ | ✓ | ✓ |
| 19 | Odisha | ✓ | ✓ | ✓ | ✓ | ✓ | ✓ | ✓ | ✓ | ✓ |
| 20 | Punjab | X | X | ✓ | ✓ | ✓ | ✓ | X | ✓ | X |
| 21 | Rajasthan | X | ✓ | ✓ | ✓ | ✓ | ✓ | X | ✓ | ✓ |
| 22 | Sikkim | X | X | ✓ | ✓ | ✓ | ✓ | X | ✓ | X |
| 23 | Tamil Nadu | X | ✓ | ✓ | ✓ | ✓ | ✓ | ✓ | ✓ | X |
| 24 | Telangana | X | X | ✓ | ✓ | ✓ | ✓ | ✓ | ✓ | X |
| 25 | Tripura | ✓ | ✓ | ✓ | ✓ | ✓ | ✓ | ✓ | ✓ | ✓ |
| 26 | Uttar Pradesh | X | ✓ | ✓ | ✓ | ✓ | ✓ | ✓ | ✓ | ✓ |

*(Contd)*

*Table 4.5 (Contd)*

| S. no. | State/UT | Limiting regulation within APMC. yard | Separation of powers between Dir (Mktg) and MD, Mandi Board | Single unified trading licence | Single-point levy of market fee | Private wholesale market | Direct marketing (outside mandi) | Declaring warehouse, silos / cold storages as deemed market | e-trading | Deregulation of marketing of fruits and vegetables |
|---|---|---|---|---|---|---|---|---|---|---|
| 27 | Uttarakhand | ✓ | ✓ | ✓ | ✓ | ✓ | ✓ | ✓ | ✓ | ✓ |
| 28 | West Bengal | X | X | ✓ | ✓ | ✓ | ✓ | X | ✓ | ✓ |
| 29 | Delhi | X | X | X | X | X | X | X | X | ✓ |
| 30 | Chandigarh | X | X | ✓ | ✓ | ✓ | ✓ | X | ✓ | X |
| 31 | Puducherry | X | X | ✓ | ✓ | ✓ | ✓ | ✓ | ✓ | ✓ |
| 32 | Jammu & Kashmir | | | | | | | | | |
| 33 | Ladakh | | | | | | | | | |
| 34 | A&N Islands | | | | | NO APMC Act | | | | |
| 35 | DNH | | | | | | | | | |
| 36 | Daman & Diu | | | | | | | | | |
| 37 | Lakshadweep | | | | | | | | | |

*Note*: ✓ means—Yes, X means—No

*Source*: Directorate of Marketing & Inspection, Ministry of Agriculture and Farmers' Welfare, Government of India. Available at https://dmi.gov.in/Documents/Reform_Status.pdf (accessed August 2023).

Even as recently as 2019, the Fifteenth Finance Commission's report for 2020–21 introduced performance-based grants for states to incentivise them to adopt the Model APLM Act, 2017, the Model Agricultural Produce and Livestock Contract Farming and Services (Promotion and Facilitation) Act, 2018 (APLCFSA or Contract Farming Act), and the Model Land Leasing Act (Rawal et al. 2020). The only issue which was somewhat unresolved is the wide variation in market fees and cesses across states (Table 4.6).

Acharya and Mehrotra (2020) are of the view that given the limited infrastructure and imperfect information base, it is not certain that full potential of perfect and competitive markets can be exploited. They also question whether partnership between small farmers and agri-business firms will work as the two are not equals. Further, the hinterlands can be integrated into the national market only if huge investments are made over the years but it is not clear who and why would one make this investment. They also draw attention to the ecological implications of opening of agricultural markets in the context of waste of non-renewables like fossil fuel and water. They conclude that rather than a 'shock treatment' of the sector, the 2019 recommendations of the Committee on doubling farmers' incomes needed implementation. They recognise the growing disparity between farm and non-farm incomes and premise their analysis on a few non-negotiables which include food security, farmer income, lower inequality, and ecological protection.

Acharya and Mehrotra (2020) point out that the MSP system which came in during the early 1960s and where farmers responded to higher prices had to be recommended by a USAID expert, as farmers were then selling their crops at very low prices at the time of harvest. They assess the problems of the APMC mandi system in terms of the changing profile of agricultural produce from crop to non-crop, the many ills of the APMC functioning,

**Table 4.6: State/UT-wise details of market fee/cess being collected by APMCs**

| *Name of the state/UT* | *Rate of market fees in percent,* ad valorem | *Cess* |
|---|---|---|
| Andhra Pradesh | 1.0 (except fish: 0.5 and prawn: 0.25) | Nil |
| Arunachal Pradesh | 2.0 | Nil |
| Assam | 1.0 | Nil |
| Chhattisgarh | Fruits and vegetables: Nil<br>Paddy: 2.0<br>Other commodities: 1.0 | Nil |
| Goa | 1.0 | Nil |
| Gujarat | Perishables: 0.5–1.0<br>Food grains: 0.3–2.0 | Nil |
| Haryana | Fruits and vegetables: Nil<br>Other commodities: 2.0<br>Cotton: 0.8 | 1 per cent Rural Development Fund Cess<br>2 per cent Rural Development Fund Cess<br>Auction fee: Rs 0.08 per hundred rupees |
| Himachal Pradesh | 1.0 | Nil |
| Jammu and Kashmir | Nil | Market fee is not collected. However, gate entry fee is collected from the selected markets of Narwal, Parimpora, Sopore, Kulgram, Shopian, and Pulwana. |
| Jharkhand | 1.0 | Nil |
| Karnataka | Perishables: 1.0–1.5 as service charge<br>Others: 1.5 | Nil |
| Madhya Pradesh | 2.0 (except orange and banana: 1.0) | Nirashrit Shulk: 0.2 per cent cess |
| Maharashtra | 0.5–1.0 | 0.05 Supervision Fee |
| Meghalaya | 1 | Nil |
| Mizoram | Ground rent: Rs 5.0 per sq. ft. | Nil |
| Nagaland | Market fee: Rs 2 per quintal as service charge | Nil |

*(Contd)*

*Table 4.6 (Contd)*

| *Name of the state/UT* | *Rate of market fees in percent,* ad valorem | *Cess* |
|---|---|---|
| Odisha | Perishables: 1.0<br>Food grains (Paddy: 2.0 and remaining: 1.0) | Nil |
| Punjab | 2.0<br>(Cotton: 1.0,<br>for primary trade: 3.0) | Rural Development Cess: 2.0 per cent |
| Rajasthan | F & V: user charge<br>Jowar, bajra, maize, isabgol, cumin: 1.0<br>Other Commodities: 1.6 | Nil |
| Tamil Nadu | 1.0 | Nil |
| Telangana | 1.0 (except fish: 0.5, prawn 0.25) | Nil |
| Tripura | 2.0 | Nil |
| Uttar Pradesh | 2.0 | Development Cess: 0.5 per cent |
| Uttarakhand | Fruits and vegetables: 1.0<br>Others: 2.0 | Development Cess: 0.5 per cent |
| West Bengal | Perishables: Nil<br>Paddy: 1.0 (6.0 for specific buyers)<br>Other than paddy: 0.5 | Nil |
| Chandigarh | 2.0 on all agricultural produce (except maize: 1.0) | Rural Development Cess: 2.0 per cent |
| Delhi | 1.0 | Entry fee charged depending upon the type of vehicle |
| Puducherry | 1.0 | Nil |

*Source*: LSS (2019).

and imposition of many restrictions on market players, besides ill-effects of MSP-based procurement system in terms of wastage of foodgrains and overuse of natural resources like water. They recognise that the inter-state movement of agricultural produce is restricted, auctions are not transparent, and payments are delayed. They conclude that the MSP mandi regime, in its present form, has outlived its utility. However, they dispute the government contention that the new laws would have enabled doubling of farmer income by 2022 and state that with the Covid-19 situation, these claims have been shelved. They question the various provisions of the new Acts on the ground that full opening up of markets without controls is similar to state withdrawal from the sector, and fear that the APMC system might fade away in a purely market-determined regime. Further, the rationale for opening up of the sector to reduce fiscal burden on the government is found to be inadequate. They ask whether Indian small farmers will be able to access the brave new larger electronic or other markets or if we are headed for pre-Sir Chhotu Ram days.[1]

Acharya and Mehrotra (2020) also question Chand (2020)'s recommendation of fixing the market fee at 1.5 per cent without considering the APMC market turnover which is likely to come down after the coming in of new channels. They argue that if the mandi fee is removed, it will have non-fiscal implications like the essence of a federal structure in a diverse country, which should not be ignored as it would increase the dependence of the states on the Union government. They fear that if a central law is not followed by the states or rather reversed partly or fully in their assemblies, this would be a first in India and can raise serious issues on the Constitution and the federal structure. They find that there is a trust deficit between farmers and the state so far as assurances on MSP and procurement are concerned. They also consider the comparison with non–MSP-protected crops as the example for benefits from private markets to be wishful thinking because oilseeds are being purchased through the mandis, and sugarcane and cotton are purchased through the cooperatives and Cotton Corporation of India, respectively. They also find issues with the dispute resolution mechanism and the exclusionary practice of contract farming, which can lead to higher differentiation among farmers and rising inequality. In fact, the leasing out of lands by the farmers to corporates and other farmers would lead them to become wage workers on their own land or elsewhere, and this is already emerging in many parts of India. Therefore, they suggest a law which ensures guaranteed, predictable, and remunerative price for all crops for farmers and believe that if price regulation is fully done away with for all crops, the situation would only worsen. They even endorse the recommendation of a committee of state ministers that complete deregulation of market does not help in attracting private investment. The concerns of net foodgrain-buying households like manual labourers and other low-earning people in the non-farm sector should also be considered since food may become expensive because of these Acts. They conclude that a vast and diverse country with multiple agroclimatic zones, demographic pressures, and land management systems cannot be governed by 'one size fit[s] all shock solutions' (Acharya and Mehrotra 2020: 26).

In fact, though dispute resolution was always outside the purview of the civil courts even under the APMC Acts, the SC Committee surprisingly recommended that an alternative mechanism for dispute settlement via civil courts or arbitration may be provided to stakeholders (SC Committee 2021), which was completely unnecessary and would not be fruitful for farmers given the complexity of this system and delay involved. The only other somewhat useful recommendation the Committee offered so far as the FPTC Act was concerned was an additional document as an alternative to the PAN card. But what was needed was to ensure some counterparty risk, which entailed more than requiring an ID proof, and making sure that the farmer could be compensated if a buyer defaulted on payment. The APMC system had this in the form of a licence and bank guarantees from buyers. In fact, the Committee report went beyond its mandate when it proposed policy measures like an agricultural marketing council under the Minister of Agriculture on the lines of GST council.

Paradoxically, although the basic objective of the new Acts was to open up agricultural markets for both buyers and farmer sellers, the Union Acts would have brought re-regulation in some states. For instance, Bihar had done away with regulation a long time ago, while Sikkim and Kerala never had any. This goes against the argument for freeing of markets, though that need not be desirable, as the experience of Bihar shows (Bera 2021; Singh 2015).

## Why were Farmers and Arthiyas Protesting? Would APMCs have Disappeared?

It is important to note that the MSP-based public procurement regime has been very unfair to some farmers and some states, and mostly benefits a few crops like wheat, paddy, and cotton in Punjab, Haryana, Madhya Pradesh, Telangana, Chhattisgarh, Uttar Pradesh, and Odisha. This represents not even 10 per cent of India's farming households: because most of them are counted double in typical data, as they grow both wheat and paddy. However, it is true that the list of MSP-based procurement states has expanded, due to decentralised procurement of farm produce, now encompassing 15 states (Gupta et al. 2020). But, most of the small and marginal farmers in these and many other states are still left out of the public procurement net.

There was a (mis)perceived linkage between the new APMC mandi bypass Act, and the MSP-based public procurement system, namely the belief that MSP-based procurement by the government would not have continued once this Act came into force. It is important to recognise that the MSP and procurement system are policy issues and not legal ones, unlike the APMC mandi bypass Act. The fear being expressed by farmers and their unions about MSP and public procurement arises from the fact that the playing field between the new trade area and APMC market buyers was unequal since there were no taxes in the new trade area, whereas there are significant buying costs in APMC-mandi based purchases, going as high as 8.5 per cent in Punjab, including 2.5 per cent commission for the commission agents (the arthiyas). Therefore, due to the lower buying cost, traders and agents might have moved out of the APMC market yards and started buying in the new trade (non-APMC) area. The Union government agencies like FCI and CCI could also proactively shift (as is being planned according to media reports) to the new trade area to buy directly from farmers. This would would have given access to MSP for farmers but the arthiyas could have suffered, as they would not be able to charge commissions which increase with every hike in MSP (Singh 2020a). In fact, after the new Acts, for the first time, CCI bought cotton in Punjab directly from farmers in APMC mandis without paying commission to the arthiyas. If the APMC mandi declined as a channel due to this new Act, then what would be the source of reference for price for private buyers in the new trade area? Also, what would have happened to the argument then that the central Act was more about giving choice of channels to farmers as there would be only private market channel without any mechanism to discover prices competitively unlike with an auction system in the APMC mandi?

That existing APMC mandis were likely to face a crisis after the new Act came into force was clear from the then available reports, which suggested that trade was moving outside the APMCs, and state governments were owering the market fees and other cesses to retain some competitive position, as illustrated by the case of

Madhya Pradesh (Arora 2020; Dwary 2021; Kakvi 2020; Siddique 2020).

Surprisingly, instead of attending to this concern, the SC Committee recommended abolishing the market fees in APMCs altogether to create a level playing field between new trade area and the APMCs! It further suggested a compensation fund to the states for three to five years for the revenue loss on the lines of GST revenue (SC Committee 2021).

The performance of the APMC mandis in Madhya Pradesh after new Acts came in shows to some extent the likely impact of new Union Acts on this kind of infrastructure and institution:

(i) 47 mandis out of 269 mandis and 298 sub-mandis recorded no business in October 2020.

(ii) Another 143 mandis recorded 40–60 per cent drop in business during June to October 2020. Only 79 mandis were functional (mostly fruit and vegetable mandis) which deal in produce denotified from APMC regulation.

(iii) Average drop in revenue in October 2020 compared with the previous year was 20.4 per cent (range: 4–71 per cent).

(iv) State mandi board revenue fell by 64 per cent compared with that in 2019.

(v) Farm produce was selling at prices half of MSP except wheat. Major reasons for decline in revenue: Covid-19, lower soyabean production, reduction of mandi fee from 1.5 per cent to 0.5 per cent after the enactment of the Central Act in September and the New Acts.

(vi) State mandi board employees have asked government to absorb 9000 employees in the state government offices.

(vii) Despite the new Acts making inter-state trade free for farmers and buyers, the state did not allow other state farmers to sell in its mandis to avail of MSP.

Of course, there is no denying that there could be some Covid-19 impact here as well. Even in Gujarat, a large number of APMCs (35) have been reported to be having no business despite having physical market yard, and the state proposes to invest in them (GoG 2021).

Farmers' and other stakeholders' apprehension about MSP and procurement going away also came from the 2020 Acts being linked to some previous policy documents, such as the Shanta Kumar Committee Report of 2015 (HLC 2015) and the Commission for Agricultural Costs and Prices (CACP) reports, which suggested reduced procurement and an end to open-ended procurement from states like Punjab to cut down buying costs of FCI. It was feared that FCI itself may start procuring directly from the new trade area to cut down its buying costs, especially market fees and arthiya commissions. In effect, it were the changes in the 'social contract' between the state's farmers and the Union government which was the root cause of this apprehension.

For commission agents, the more problematic aspect of the new Acts was as follows: they typically interlock handling of the farm produce with cash-and-kind credit to farmers for various purposes and recover their loans from such sales proceeds of farmers in the APMC market (Shah 2021; Singh 2021). In fact, in Punjab, the payments for farmer produce are made to the arthiyas, not the farmers, even by FCI and CCI, and this has been an issue for at least two decades. The state government has not allowed the central agencies to pay directly to farmers for various political economy reasons, including the power of the arthiya lobby, as well as many of the commission agents being also large farmers who hold power in the state government and its agencies. The state government also opposed a March 2021 central directive of the FCI to its food and civil supplies department to pay directly to farmers in their bank accounts, and citing the practice of large-scale (informal) leased land-based cultivation of crops which cannot be identified with land records of sellers as they are not owners and also reasoning that farmers cannot do without credit from the arthiyas. The arthiyas were then being described as a 'necessary evil', essential to the APMC mandi system, or as service providers (Sinha 2020). Of course, the arthiyas might get into a new role of being facilitators or agents of corporates in the new trade area. But they would not have been able to interlock the credit and produce or input markets as in an APMC mandi and would have had to be satisfied with lower commissions. However, it might still not mean that the buyers in the new trade area would pass on even a part of the lower buying cost to the selling farmers in the form of higher produce purchase prices (Singh 2020d). Nevertheless, it can be argued that the disintermediation in farm produce markets, which means removing the arthiyas, has been long overdue: indeed, Madhya Pradesh made that move as long ago as in 1985.

The 2020 directive of the FCI to the Government of Punjab to arrange to pay farmers directly for their produce bought by the FCI in Punjab into their bank accounts and not through the CAs is a clear signal that the central agencies are not keen to maintain the arthiya as an intermediary. The FCI is reported to have even offered to pass on the 2.5 per cent commission earlier paid to the arthiyas, to the farmers in their accounts as an incentive for receiving direct payment. However, the FCI would still buy from the APMC mandis like how the CCI did in case of cotton during the Kharif season without involving and paying the arthiyas.

The Bihar experience is a significant lesson in how not to open up markets or reform agricultural markets. In Bihar, paddy procurement targets were 30 lakh metric tonne, only 19 per cent of total production during 2013–14 to 2015–16, but only 41–80 per cent of the target was met, despite having 8436 PACS (Primary Agricultural Credit Societies) and VMSSs (Vyapar Mandal Sahyog Samitis) in the state (Kumar 2020). Even after 14 years of no APMC regulation, paddy (interlocked) price was found to be Rs 1100 per quintal against MSP of Rs 1868, and the cost of production: Rs 1245. Purchase centres declined from 9035 in 2015–16 to 7000 in 2018–19 and only 1619 in 2019–20. There was no procurement of wheat by PACS or there were delayed payments, and there were no weigh bridges with them. Further, post-2006, FHP (Farm Harvest Prices) of paddy was lower than MSP during all years, especially during 2014–15 to 2016–17 by more than Rs 143–297 per quintal. There was a much lower difference pre-2006 (Rs 73–120). The case of wheat was no different with difference of Rs 61–326 vs. Rs 80–103 earlier, and for maize as well (Rs 70–259 vs Rs 17–102 earlier). The fluctuation of prices (instability, i.e., CV or Coefficient of Variation) in this difference between paddy MSP and FHP and of wholesale prices also doubled post-2006. The abolition of the Act led to not 'freedom' for farmers, but 'free fall' for farmers as the deregulation (repeal of the APMC Act) created a vacuum in the marketplace without any alternatives. Finally, price effect on crop output growth which was highly positive became negative in post-2006 period; net income from paddy (already negative) became six times lower (Singh and Kumar 2020); and cost of marketing which was 9.9 per cent in 1993–94 increased to 11.45 per cent in 2014–15; and (modified) marketing efficiency came down from 354 to 290 with farmer net price coming down from 78 per cent in 1993–94 to 74.4 per cent of consumer/retail price in 2014–15 (Kumar 2020). In private local F&V markets, farmers paid 2 per cent commission/fee which was not the case earlier; no open auction process was followed; and no private markets/channels of any significance came up.

More importantly, from the viewpoint of the farmers, perceived changes in the 'social contract' between farmers in some states and the Union government were at the root of the apprehensions which resulted in protests and their unyielding positions. This social contract was seen in the form of the government not only promising farmers an MSP for 23 crops but also procuring some of them (mainly wheat and paddy) since the 1960s, and farmers responding to it by adopting new varieties and investing in farming, which led to sufficient production of foodgrains in India over the decades.

The farmers feared that the government was not keen to stay committed to this promise and its delivery because it was providing a bigger space and role for private players in this domain. Besides, the proposals like deficiency price payment (DPP) without direct procurement by government, and suggested reduction in public procurement by some government bodies like CACP and other committees like Shanta Kumar Committee were also behind such somewhat well-founded fears.

In the popular understanding of the farmers, the role of the state would transform from that of a supportive framework for the agricultural sector to that which facilitates, even encourages corporate operations. That the state did promote contract farming directly and indirectly in India was clear from the many policy changes like allowing priority sector credit for contracting agencies instead of directly to farmers and providing incentives for contract farming, and the experience of Punjab wherein the state directly engaged in promotion of contract farming (Shrimali 2021). This was more like a fear of withdrawal of the state from agricultural markets suddenly and leaving it open to the private sector to engage with farmers, without adequate protection of the law or support of the state agencies for farmers.

## Punjab's Half–hearted APMC Mandi Act Amendments of 2017 and 2020

Punjab claimed that Entries 14 (agriculture), 18 (land rights; land tenure including tenancy relations and collection of rent; transfer and alienation of agricultural land; land improvement; agricultural loans and colonisation), Entries 28 and 27 (production, supply, and distribution of goods) of the State List were about state domain. These read with Entry 33 of the Concurrent List were relevant in the context of agricultural market law making, and therefore, the state amended the Central Acts at its level and forwarded the same to the state governor, but there was no further action after that.

Punjab tried to undo the central reform of agricultural markets with the amendment bills but ended up mainly focusing on paddy and wheat prices by making MSP the minimum purchase price for any buyer in any channel, penalising any violation of that restriction, as discussed earlier. In doing so, the state government was clearly seeking to protect its own revenue, along with other objectives. However, farmers producing other crops, such as cotton or oilseeds, or even maize, for which there is an MSP-based procurement provision from the Union government, do not receive protection under this bill (GoP 2020). This is despite the fact that cotton and maize have been selling at below MSP in the state during the 2020–21 season. It is unfortunate that the thinking of the state government did not go beyond wheat and paddy. The MSP is declared for 23 crops, but none of the other crops' farmers, or those trying to diversify under CF would have the MSP protection of the new bills.

On the issue of enforcement of MSP for all buyers, Punjab's APMC mandi bypass Act amendment bill made buying below MSP an offence which would be punishable with a term of imprisonment of not less than three years and a fine. But why would a buyer compel or exert pressure on seller farmers and how would that be established? It is more likely that a farmer would be more than willing to sell below MSP, since once the farmer brings produce to the market, it is difficult to take it back—it would be like taking a dead body back home from the cremation ground (Singh 2020c).

Even earlier, while amending the APMC Act in 2017, and framing rules for it in 2020, Punjab provided for special market yards, private market yards, producer market yards (Kisan Mandi) and producer-consumer market yards (PCMY). With regard to the setting up of private wholesale market yards, which gave for the first time a choice of a public and a private mandi for the farmer seller, the Act stated 'Provided that the above yard can be established only for the business relating to all crops other than wheat and paddy; and cannot be established within a radius of five kilometers from the existing notified principal or sub-market yards' (GoP 2017: 58). This restriction applies to the other two markets, that is, PCMY and Kisan Mandi as well (ibid.: 5). This provision shows that Punjab had protected its arthiyas and traders (*kuchcha* and *pucca* arthiyas, respectively) in the existing APMC mandis, as most of them deal in foodgrains (wheat and paddy) and cotton which are crops mostly bought by public agencies, that is, FCI and CCI. By excluding these crops from the new market arrangements, the arthiyas' vested interest was largely left untouched by the amended Punjab Act of 2017 (Singh 2020d).

So far as direct payment to the farmer seller—a long-pending and serious issue in Punjab—was concerned, the Act stated:

> The Kacha Arhtia (commission agent) or the buyer, as the case may be, shall make payment to the seller through electronic transfer after the weighment is over. If payment is not made by the *Kacha Arhtia* or buyer, as the case may be, in the manner, as stated above, then the same shall be recovered by the market committee

> concerned from him as arrears of land revenue and the first lien shall be of seller's right and it shall be made to the seller concerned (Singh 2020g).
>
> Provided further that the seller shall be at liberty to receive payment up to rupees ten thousand in cash in a calendar month for the agricultural produce sold by him during that month … Delivery of agricultural produce after sale shall not be made or taken unless and until the Kacha Arhtia or, if the seller does not employ a *Kacha Arhtia*, the buyer has given to the seller a sale voucher in Form J mentioning the payment mode and its authentication, the counterfoil of which shall be retained by the *Kacha Arhtia* or the buyer, as the case may be (Singh 2020g: 20–21).

This was more about retaining payment to farmers through the arthiya despite the issue being alive for more than 10 years by the time the Act was amended.

Thus, the analysis of the APMC mandi bypass Act 2020 and related state-level amendments shows that the Act is not only inadequate in many ways to protect farmer interest but also lacks adequate rationale for being enacted as it is based on many false assumptions and half-truths.

## Note

1. Sir Chhotu Ram was the revenue minister of Punjab during the 1930s, who introduced many farmer-friendly agricultural market reforms at that time.

## References

Acharya, S., and S. Mehrotra. 2020. 'The Agriculture Market Reforms: Is There a Trade-off Between Efficiency and Equality?' IHD Working Paper 2/2020. New Delhi: IHD.

Arora, S. 2020. 'By amending Model Mandi Act, MP has pushed its agricultural sector into throes of uncertainty', *Indian Express*, 21 December. Available at https://indianexpress.com/article/opinion/columns/madhya-pradesh-farmers-mandi-act-7113824/ (accessed July 2023).

Bera, S. 2021. 'What trade freedom did to Bihar farmers', *Mint,* 8 March. Ahmedabad.

Burman A., I. Patnaik, S. Roy, and A. Shah. 2018. 'Diagnosing and Overcoming Sustained Food Price Volatility: Enabling a National Market for Food', NIPFP Working Paper No. 236, 3 May, New Delhi.

Chand, R. 2020. *New Farm Acts: Understanding the Implications*. New Delhi: National Institution for Transforming India (NITI), GoI, November.

Dwary, A. 2021. 'Madhya Pradesh *Mandis'* Revenue at One–Third in January, To Rent Out Space', *NDTV*, 12 February.

GoG (Government of Gujarat). 2021. *Atmanirbhar Farmers of Gujarat: Roadmap 2030*. Gandhinagar: Government of Gujarat, December.

GoP (Government of Punjab). 2017. *The Punjab Agricultural Produce Markets Act, 1961* (Punjab Act No. 23 of 1961), substituted by *The Punjab Agricultural Produce Markets (Second Amendment) Act, 2017* (Punjab Act No. 17 of 2017 dated 14.8.17).

______. 2020. *The Farmers' Produce Trade and Commerce, (Promotion and Facilitation) (Special Provisions and Punjab Amendment) Bill, 2020,* Punjab Vidhan Sabha Bill No. 32-PLA-2020, Government of Punjab.

GoR (Government of Rajasthan). 2020. *The Farmers' Produce Trade and Commerce (Promotion And Facilitation) (Rajasthan Amendment) Bill, 2020*, Bill No. 30 of 2020, Government of Rajasthan, p. 4.

Gopikuttam, G. S., and G. Naik. 2020. 'Deregulation of Agricultural Markets in India', WP No. 631/2020, IIM Bangalore.

Gupta, P., R. Khera, and S. Narayanan. 2020. 'MSP–The Factoids versus the Facts', *The Hindu*, 19 December.

HLC (High Level Committee). 2015. *Report of the High Level Committee on Reorienting the Role and Restructuring of Food Corporation of India*, New Delhi, January.

Kakvi, K. 2020. 'New laws paralyse 70 per cent of MP's Mandis in six months', *News Click,* 7 December.

Kumar, M. 2021. 'Foodstuffs Market Regulation: The Essential Commodities (amendment) Act, 2020 and After'. *Economic and Political Weekly* 56(49): 15–19.

Kumar, S. 2020. 'Efficiency of Paddy/Rice Marketing in the Post APMC Era in Bihar'. *Indian Journal of Agricultural Marketing* 34(10): 16–25.

Kumar, T. N. 2022. *Farmers, Farm Laws and Ways Forward*, Report for the Food and Land Use Coalition India, New Delhi.

LSS (Lok Sabha Secretariat). 2019. *Agriculture Marketing and Role of Weekly Gramin Haats*, Standing Committee on Agriculture, 62nd Report, 3 January, p. 12.

MoAFW. 2020. *The Farmers Produce Trade and Commerce (Promotion and Facilitation) Bill*, No. 10 of 2020, Ministry of Agriculture and Farmer Welfare (MoAFW), Government of India.

MPSAMB. 2005. *MP Krish Upaj Mandi Adhiniyam*, 1972 (MP Act No. 24 of 1973), up to date amended Act. Bhopal: MPSAMB.

Narayanan, S. 2020. 'The Three Farm Bills', *The India Forum*, 2 October.

*NDTV*. 2020. 'Day After Farm Bills Become Law, UP Farmers Stopped At Haryana Border', 29 September. Available at https://www.ndtv.com/india-news/day-after-farm-bills-become-law-50-up-farmers-stopped-at-haryana-border-2302386 (accessed August 2023).

NSO. 2021. *Situation Assessment of Agricultural Households and Land and Livestock Holdings of Households in Rural India, 2019*, September. New Delhi: Ministry of Statistics and Programme Implementation, Government of India.

Rawal, V., S. Patel, and J. Pais. 2020. *The Political Economy of Agricultural Market Reforms—An Analysis of the Farmers' Produce Trade and Commerce (Promotion and Facilitation) Act, 2020*, SSER monograph No. 20/4. New Delhi: SSER.

SC Committee. 2021. *Report of the Supreme Court Appointed Committee on Farm Laws*, March, Supreme Court of India.

Shah, M. 2021. 'Mere Paas Sarkaar Hai', *The India Forum*, 5 February.

Shrimali, R. 2021. *Contract Farming, Capital and State: Corporatisation of Indian Agriculture*. Singapore: Palgrave Macmillan.

Shylendra, H. S. 2022. 'Ingenious Farmers and Ignoble Experts: Case of the Supreme Court Appointed Committee on Farm Laws'. *Mainstream* LX (24).

Siddique, I. 2020. 'Amid New Farm Laws, Pandemic, Madhya Pradesh Mandis Take a Hit', *Indian Express*, 14 December.

Singh, G. 2020. 'Agribusiness Supply Chains: Smallholder Participation and Implications', PhD thesis, Lincoln University. New Zealand: Christchurch.

Singh, S. 2015. 'Reforming markets, lessons from Bihar', *The Tribune*, 6 February. Chandigarh, Op ed., Agriculture.

———. 2018a. 'APMCs: The other side of the story', *The Hindu Business Line*, 24 January, Opinion.

———. 2018b. 'Reforming Agricultural markets in India: A tale of two model Acts'. *Economic and Political Weekly* 53(51): 44–49.

———. 2020a. 'Agricultural Market Reforms during Covid-19 Times: Will They Make any Difference?' In Sunil Mani, Alok Sheel, R. Nagaraj, Sukhpal Singh, P. S. Vijayshankar, S. Irudaya Rajan, P. L. Beena, M. Parameswaran, and Chidambaran G. Iyer (eds), *The Stimulus Package in Five Instalments: Does It Make the Economy More Self-Reliant?*, CDS Commentary on India's Economy and Society series, No. 15, June. Thiruvananthapuram: CDS.

———. 2020b. 'Tale of two flawed agri ordinances', *The Hindu Business Line*, 21 June, Opinion.

Singh, S. 2020c. 'Farm laws: Design leaves much to be desired', 13 October, *Ideas for India*.

———. 2020d. 'Farmers' freedom at stake', 23 October, *Frontline*, 27–31.

———. 2020e. 'Farmers' Apprehensions about Role of Mandis, Terms of Procurement under New Laws Need to be Addressed', *The Indian Express*, 3 December.

———. 2020f. 'Ownership v/s Control: The Changing Dynamics of Land Use in Liberalised Agricultural Context of India'. In Deepak K. Mishra and Pradeep Nayak (eds), *Land and Livelihoods in Neoliberal India*, 57–70. Singapore: Palgrave Macmillan.

———. 2020g. 'Amending Agri Market Law, but Half-heartedly', *The Tribune*, Chandigarh.

———. 2021. 'Food Security and Markets: Understanding the Protests over India's Changing Social Contract with Farmers', *The Hindu Centre for Politics and Public Policy*, 15 March. Available at https://www.thehinducentre.com/the-arena/current-issues/article34060554.ece (accessed August 2023).

Singh, S., and S. Kumar. 2020. *Agri-Market Reforms in Bihar: Future Concerns for Indian Agriculture*, Report for Punjab Mandi Board. Ludhiana: Punjab Agricultural University.

five

# The Union Contract Farming Act, 2020*

## Issues and Implications

It is important to recognise that contract faming has been in practice in India since the 1960s in the seed sector and in other farm produce in many states, such as Punjab and Haryana, to name just two. Since the 1990s, multinationals like PepsiCo have undertaken tomato and potato contract farming in these states. There is a widespread practice of contract farming across crops, states, and agencies (public, private, and multinational) in India, covering dozens of crops and livestock products with hundreds of contract farming projects or schemes, for domestic processing or for export. It is estimated that more than 0.5 million farmers work under contracts across states and crops in India (Cariappa et al. 2023). There have been dozens of studies over the last 20 years on its performance and experience. Contract farming has been permitted in most states as per the Model APMC Act, 2003

*An earlier version of a part of this chapter was published online by The Hindu Centre for Politics and Public Policy in March 2021 (Singh 2021c). An updated version of The Hindu Centre article was later published in the *Economic and Political Weekly* (Singh 2022). The present chapter has been reproduced here in a revised form with the kind permission of The Hindu Centre for Politics and Public Policy and *Economic and Political Weekly*.

of the MoAFW wherein three new channels of selling and buying farm produce—direct purchase, contract farming, and private wholesale markets—were made legal. Most states adopted this within a few years, with one or two exceptions, and later, under the Model Agricultural Produce and Livestock Marketing (Promotion and Facilitation) (APLM) Act, 2017 as well as the separate Model Agricultural Produce and Livestock Contract Farming and Services (Promotion and Facilitation) (APLCFS) Act, 2018. As mentioned earlier, Punjab was the only state which, in 2013, framed a separate Act on contract farming instead of providing for it under the APMC Act, which it had not amended adequately until 2017. However, this separate Contract Farming Act (which was technically not needed) was never operationalised.

Tamil Nadu was the first state to pass a Contract Farming Act, the Tamil Nadu Agricultural Produce and Livestock Contract Farming and Services (Promotion and Facilitation) Act, 2019 (GoTN 2019) based on the Model APLCFS Act, 2018, and Odisha did the same in 2020.

For buyers, contract farming is the only other option in India outside of buying from APMCs or private wholesale markets, and direct purchase as the corporate farming option is simply not available in India due to the Ceilings on Land Holdings Acts, under which non-agriculturists cannot own agricultural land, and the Land Leasing Act, under which they cannot even lease in agricultural land, both Acts having been passed at the state level. Hence, if a company wants to procure desired quality raw material or farm produce in adequate quantity at a reasonable cost, which may not be available in the open market or not even be grown by farmers, for example, processing variety (chips grade) potatoes in India before Pepsi came in; then contract farming is the only option in India, and this is what Pepsi used. For farmers, contract farming can potentially bring not only assured market and price but also new technology, seeds, extension services, and such other non-price benefits (Singh 2020h).

But, contract farmers in various parts of India have faced many problems like undue deductions in quality assessment on produce by firms, or no procurement of produce, delayed deliveries at the factory, delayed payments, low-price, poor-quality inputs, no compensation for crop failure or unexpectedly high cost of production, and even stagnation of contract prices over time, known as 'agribusiness normalisation.' Defaulting has been an issue on both sides (companies and farmers) (Singh 2020h), and exclusion of small producers remains a major issue as well (Singh 2012). That contract farming has been problematic globally is underscored by the recent FAO initiative on promoting responsible contract farming (FAO and IISD 2018).

It has also led to regionally uneven spread as contracting agencies tend to work in some regions like Andhra Pradesh or Punjab which are seen more favourable to such arrangement unlike others like West Bengal (Shrimali 2021). It is not incidental that most of the contract farming projects are in the states of Punjab, Haryana, Gujarat, Maharashtra, Karnataka, and Tamil Nadu which are agriculturally developed states. On the other hand, vast areas of India such as Bihar, Jharkhand, Chhattisgarh, Odisha, West Bengal, the entire north-east India, and areas of Uttarakhand, Himachal Pradesh, Kerala, and Jammu and Kashmir have been bypassed by contract farming projects. Does it mean that these areas and farmers would not benefit from commercialisation and vertical co-ordination of agriculture? These are areas with the highest concentration of small and marginal farmers (Gill 2004). This essentially means that contracting companies do not encourage participation of those who need to be helped to participate since risk preference and innovativeness require not just an attitude adjustment like the agriculturally developed states, but also resources and risk-taking capability to undertake risky crops and ventures (Glover 1987). This has potential to contribute to already existing regional inequalities and levels of deprivation and prosperity across states and regions.

The agro-input companies and banking sector also join hands in perpetuation of contract farming practice as they leverage it for input selling and extending credit without much risk through the contracting companies, instead of selling farm inputs or credit to individual farmers. Contracting companies recommend only certain inputs and of certain brands and types, which helps partner input companies to get a secure market for their products. This makes corporatisation of the sector even more widespread and permanent (Shrimali 2021). Besides the regulatory aspects which promote corporatisation of the farm sector which is the focus of this book, the other measures are more in the nature of policy like the agricultural export policy, national policy for farmers, and banking sector reforms and liberalisation which bring in the corporate agribusiness players into the farm sector through mechanisms like contract farming, described as the 'great Indian thali'[1] by Shrimali (ibid.). Contract farming also lets corporates control land and farm production without owning land and, therefore, avoids direct investments in land which maybe risky and not viable, and thus helps accumulation without dispossession (ibid.; Singh 2020a).

## Breach of Contracts and Need for Regulation

Defaults by farmers as well as firms which is a global phenomenon in contract farming (Pultrone 2012) has been reported in India too (Haque 2003; Kumar et al. 2013; Singh 2002, 2004). Though contract farming in gherkin and iceberg lettuce crop was smooth as there was no local market or very thin market for the crop, there was flexibility in contracts due to the short duration of the crops, and farmers maintained alternative sources of income (Khairnar and Yeleti 2005; Singh and Asokan 2005). But, still, there was partial breach of contracts in gherkins as the firm did not procure as per contract in case of 63 per cent of contract farmers in Andhra Pradesh. This was so only in 30 per cent cases in paddy seed contract farming (Swain 2011).

The firms also manipulated provisions of the contracts in practice; for example, in the case of broiler chickens in Tamil Nadu, they picked up birds before due date, or delayed it depending on the demand which meant losses for contract growers. They also delayed payments upto 60 days. But growers were locked into these contracts due to the specific and fixed investments they had made (Singh and Asokan 2005). In fact, broiler contract farming cannot really be representative of the contract farming in agriculture as it is more of a case of 'putting out work' or 'wage labour contracting' as the contracting agency provides all the inputs ranging from day-old chicks to feed and vaccination, and the contract grower just provides labour for feeding the birds and supervision, and land requirement is not a big factor.

## Contract Farming and Natural Resource Sustainability

Though it is known that contract farming has resulted in a transfer of responsibility for many production decisions from the individual farmer to the contracting company (Opondo 2000), it is not yet understood whether the responsibility for environmental impacts has also shifted (Rickson et al. 1993 in Eaton 1998). But there is hardly any rigorous evidence on the environmental impacts of contract farming, as the focus most of the time has been on its impact on small producer livelihoods in terms of removing poverty or risk in their activities (Minten et al. 2006).

Contract farming influences the direction of ecological change through two actors. The contracting agency lays down the production schedule for the farmers (the first actor) at the farm level. By determining the crop to be grown and the husbandry practices the farmer has to follow, the contracting agency influences the impact contract farming will have on the environment. The government is the second actor as the main source of conservation measures, that is, advisory, financial, and material. The farmer's access to these measures is, to a large extent, determined by government policy. Thus, the contracting agency and the government have a larger role to play in environmental/ ecological change than the farmer since they occupy a 'privileged' position in the realm of decision-making (Opondo 2000).

The environmental implications of contract farming include monocultures leading to depletion of soil quality, and effect of fertilisers and pesticides on natural resources, environment, humans, and animals (Opondo 2000). Environment is also impacted through rejection of some produce of the grower by the contracting agency as the cost of not harvesting results in soil loss through tillage, excessive use, and wastage of chemicals causing nutrient depletion (Lawrence 1999). The contracting firms tend to aggravate the environmental crisis as most of the contracts are short term (one or two crop cycles), and the firms tend to move on to new growers and lands after exhausting the natural potential of the local resources, particularly land and water, or when productivity declines due to some other reason (Raynolds 2000). The over-exploitation of groundwater, salination of soils, decline in soil fertility, and pollution are examples of environmental degradation due to contract farming (Rickson and Burch 1996). The firms do not pay heed as the costs of such effects are externalised so far as the firm is concerned. It is also argued that contract farming as part of the globalisation process might lead to increasing investments in developing countries, which have low environmental standards, and thus, the natural resource base might end up irreversibly depleted or damaged (Minten et al. 2006).

What comes out from the analysis of the contract farming situations is that increasingly, environmental concerns are dictated by market demand. One example is the case of chemical residues or organic practices. In Kenya, most of the environmental management efforts were influenced by consumer preferences in the industrialised countries. This led to drastic reduction in misuse and abuse of the pesticides (Opondo 2000). But markets may not signal the importance of ecological concerns in all situations and all times due to various imperfections in the market and externalities in the presence of weak monitoring. For example, in Kenya, soil erosion was not attended to by the contracting agencies as that was not reflected in the product quality and was an externality of the contract production. It continued to be seen as the responsibility of the farmer and the government (ibid.).

## Major Flaws in Contract Farming Act, 2020

The Farmers (Empowerment and Protection) Agreement on Price Assurance and Farm Services Act, 2020 (MoAFW 2020b) was nothing but a badly designed Contract Farming Act. The use of the term 'farming agreement' itself was unusual as it was being confused with other arrangements like sharecropping or leasing agreements. Contract farming is about contract first and farming being a part of it, and not just farming. The biggest problem in perception was that it was being confused with corporate farming (corporates doing their own farming on leased or owned land) and it was definitely not that. The Act clearly said that the contracting agency cannot lay any claims on the farmer's land and cannot even lease it.

However, the manner in which the production agreement was defined raised fears of land leasing being a part of it. The Act defined a production agreement as: 'Where sponsor agrees to provide farm services, either fully or partially and to bear the risk of output but agrees to make payment to the farmer for the services rendered by such farmer.'

How can this be a case of contract farming? Why would a sponsor pay a farmer for services? How can a buyer bear output (production) risk? The contracting agency only bears and reduces farmer's market risk. Therefore, it is only natural to suspect that this was about land leasing rather than contract farming.

In fact, the Rajasthan Amendment Bill, 2020 was more upfront as it accepted/assumed that leasing was legal under the Act and stated:

> Where under a farming agreement, sponsor undertakes the farming by deploying his/its manpower, the sponsor shall be liable to remove his manpower from the agriculture farm/field from the next date of termination of the farming agreement and in the event of manpower of the sponsor continuing in the agricultural farm/field, the sponsor shall be liable to pay damages to the farmer to the tune of such amount as may be notified by the state government from time to time which shall not be less than one thousand rupees per bigha per day (GoR 2020).

Even the Model APLCFS Act, 2018, had land leasing allowed under the definition of contract farming (Singh 2018), which was not correct. Going by the nature of activity which the law sought to address, contract farming, where the primacy is on production of crop by a farmer, can never include land leasing, as in the latter case, the farmer is not involved in production.

The 'trade and commerce agreement' defined as 'where the ownership of commodity remains with the farmer during production and he gets the price of produce on its delivery as per the agreed terms with the Sponsor' under the Act was nothing but direct purchase, which was not the appropriate transaction under any contract farming Act. Also, large retailers/supermarkets were mentioned as contracting parties but they only bought directly without contracts.

Section 9 of the APLCFS Act also linked contract farming with insurance and credit under any (Union or state) government scheme or any financial service provider for flow of credit for farmer/sponsor/both, which entailed credit linkage and, therefore, farmer concern about land mortgage/hypothecation. Further, recovery of sponsor loss due to force majeure (natural calamities) of just any advances was also problematic as actual costs incurred by sponsor can be quite different from services rendered to the grower. On the other hand, there was no provision in the Act for the recovery of loss to the farmer. The provision of new intermediaries like Krishi Vikas Kendras (KVKs), third party assayers, seed certification agencies, and agricultural scientists for quality assessment, service provision, and aggregation as parties was rather unnecessary, and reflected the increasing role of standards and external agencies in farmer-level decisions or in relations between contract agencies and farmers, as it would also lead to higher costs for farmers as suppliers.

The Act specifically mentioned that in case of seed contract farming, the sponsor would make payment of not less than two-third of the agreed amount at the time of delivery and the remaining after due certification, but not later than 30 days of delivery. In seed contract farming, it is well known that often, standing crops are asked to be ploughed down by the sponsor if quality seed is not expected to be produced from a given plot of land. The compensation for that is a big issue for farmers, and it was not addressed at all in the Act.

But, it specifically mentioned that quality, grade, and standards for pesticide residue, food safety, good farming practices, labour, and social development standards may also be adopted in the farming agreement. It even went to the extent of specifying third party assayers to monitor these and to ensure impartiality and fairness (Singh 2020c). It is sad that the social and labour aspects were only suggested and not made mandatory, given the fact that child labour and labour exploitation in wages and work conditions are widely prevalent in contract farming of seed and many other crops in India (Banday et al. 2018; D'Cruz et al. 2021; Singh 2008b, 2017). It was also affecting India's exports and reputation in global markets for fair trade and ethical products besides being exploitative of farm workers, especially women and female children (Singh 2020c). There were also serious violations of various laws of the land like the Child Labour Act and Minimum Wages Act in the form of exploitation of child labour, gender disparity in wages, unfair wages, and so on, which were only broadly addressed by mentioning various market-based standards, but not in terms of the laws of the land.

In the 2020 Union Act, the very basic aspects of contract farming like acreage, quantity, and time of delivery were not specified, which is a must for any law of regulation as these are mandatory aspects of such an arrangement whether with supply of inputs or otherwise. These were very clearly stated in the Model APMC 2003 Act besides optional provisions (Singh 2020c). The SC Committee recommended only a model contract farming agreement to be formulated and shared with stakeholders for removing various implementation issues (SC Committee 2021), though one is not sure how a model agreement can resolve some of the design and content issues inherent in the very Act itself.

The only other suggestion it had on this Act were about notifying a registering authority for contract agreements and provision for witnesses on both sides of the parties to the agreement.

More surprisingly, the SC Committee described the cases of direct purchase of fruits and vegetables practised by Mother Dairy, and the procurement operations of a farmer producer company as cases of contract farming. This showed the lack of appreciation of the concept of contract farming or a deliberate misinterpretation of the concept by the Committee because these types of procurement arrangements are not part of the contract farming arrangement by definition since as we have been discussing, in contract farming, a farmer is asked to grow a crop/produce and then the contracting agency buys it on a pre-agreed basis. The above cases are of direct purchase, not contract farming. Like the Contract Farming Act, they were pushing other arrangements including land leasing under the garb of contract farming, for corporate entry into agriculture.

## Poor Design and Role of Farmer Producer Organisations (FPOs)

As we have just mentioned, another flaw in the Act was that basic aspects of contract farming like acreage, quantity, and time of delivery were not specified. The government advertisement claimed that farmers could withdraw from contract arrangement anytime without incurring any penalties. This was again not true and cannot be a part of the arrangement if contract farming has to succeed. The Act also left out many sophisticated aspects of modern contract farming practice like contract cancellation clauses, delayed deliveries or purchase, and damages therein, and 'tournaments' in contract farming where farmers are made to compete with each other and paid as per relative performance, which is banned in many countries (Singh 2020b).

It is rather unfortunate that the Act linked bonus or premium price under contract arrangement over and above the guaranteed or pre-agreed price with APMC mandi price or electronic market price, which has to be part of the contract agreement. This approach is anti-contract farming in nature. The price like many other basic aspects of contract should have been left to the parties to negotiate and cannot be tied to any other channel, especially APMC price, since this would defeat the stated rationale for bringing in this law, which is to provide alternative channels to farmers and create competition for APMC markets. Having started off by asserting that these APMCs were inefficient in price discovery and yet going back to the same mandi not only speaks ill of the Act, but could also raise apprehensions over the real intent that propelled these laws.

The guidelines also allowed sharecroppers to be made a party to the contract and be held responsible for receiving and utilising the inputs as well. This is very surprising as a contract farming agreement is generally between either a landowner, or a lessee as one party, and the contracting agency as the other, and not both. The guidelines also mentioned that contract agreement should be as good as any contract under the Contract Act. If the contract farming agreement was being kept outside the purview of the civil courts, then why give this guideline? It showed a lack of clarity of the various provisions of the Act and raised questions about the rationale behind them.

Like the FPTC Act, in the Contract Farming Act too, categorising an FPO as a farmer was not proper. There are many FPOs in India which are undertaking contract farming directly or indirectly with their members and non-member farmers, like in seed production (Singh 2020a). Therefore, clubbing them with the farmers is not correct. They are more buyers and suppliers than producers.

That the Act went all the way to facilitate contract farming was clear from the fact that it mentioned that the Stock Limit Act (under the ECA) would not apply to contract-farmed produce. Why should this provision of another Act be specifically mentioned in another law, which has nothing to do with this law directly or indirectly? The Contract Farming Act guidelines even gave a role to a sharecropper as third party in the contract agreement, which was surprising. More importantly, the aspects of farmer empowerment and protection mentioned in the title of the Act was neglected in its contents.

Since the Model ALPCFS Act, 2018, land leasing has been made part of the contract farming definition, which is not accurate. The 2020 Act protected farmers' land when it stated in Section 14:

> No farming agreement shall be entered into for the purpose of (a) any transfer, including sale, lease or mortgage of the land or premises of the farmer; or (b) raising any permanent structure or making any modification on the land or premises of the farmer, unless Sponsor agrees to remove such structure or to restore the land to its original condition, at his cost, on the conclusion of the agreement or expiry of the agreement period, as the case may be (MoAFW 2020b).

But there is a problem in these provisions as some other provisions in the Act are contradictory. For example, the dispute resolution section stated: 'The amount payable under any order passed by the Sub-Divisional Authority or the Appellant Authority, as the case may be, may be recovered as arrears of land revenue.' However, then again, it stated in the next Section 15, 'Notwithstanding anything contained in Section 14, no action for recovery of any amount in pursuance of an order passed under this section, shall be initiated against the agricultural land of the farmer' (MoAFW 2020b). But this still meant it could be recovered from other assets and properties of the farmer. The confusion between contract farming and corporate farming created by the Act is so significant that the Rajasthan Amendment Bill, 2020 assumed that leasing was a part of contract farming (Singh 2020a). This provision of the Amendment Bill is an outright misunderstanding of the Contract Farming Act, 2020, as a sponsor never cultivates a farmer's field under a contract farming arrangement, in which the farmer as a producer is central to the concept.

## Punjab Amendments to the Contract Farming Act, 2020

Punjab's Contract Farming Act Amendment Bill, 2020 barred any contract agreement for wheat or paddy below the MSP announced by the Central government for that crop. It stated: 'No sale or purchase of wheat or paddy shall be valid unless the price paid for such agricultural produce under a farming agreement is equal to, or greater than, the Minimum Support Price announced by the Central Government for that crop' (GoP 2020b).

However, one would not expect any agency to undertake contract farming in these two crops in Punjab, or anywhere in India, unless it were basmati paddy or durum wheat. Punjab has some basmati contract farming but that may not be included under paddy (common rice), and the state does not grow any durum wheat. As discussed earlier, MSP is declared for 23 crops, but other crop farmers, or those trying to diversify under contract farming would not have the MSP protection of the Bills. In any case, this is a bad conception per se, as contract price should not be tied to any other price, especially state declared prices, but should be negotiated by the two parties. Furthermore, contracting is also about benefits other than price, such as yield, cost, or quality of crop. Haryana had made MSP as the minimum contract price for contracting agencies in 2005 under its APMC Act but it was for all crops where MSP was applicable. Punjab should have learned from its neighbour (Singh 2020c).

Similar to the mandi bypass Act amendment, the Contract Farming Act Amendment Bill made a contract price below MSP, or forced a farmer for the same, an offence which would be punishable with imprisonment for not less than three years and a fine. Again, the same criticism noted earlier applies. In both the amended Acts, the Punjab state government created its right to levy cesses on notified or contract-farmed agricultural produce bought, brought, or sold by a corporate agency or trader and/or on the electronic platform, as the case may be, for trade and commerce in a trade area, and this cess collection would go into a fund to run the market committee and for the welfare of farmers or other purposes related to welfare and promotion of agriculture or agriculturists and development of market infrastructure (Singh 2020c). Essentially, this extends the APMC tax regime to all other transactions.

In contrast, under Rajasthan's amendments, the state government had proposed to enforce stock limits in respect of any agricultural produce under contract agreement, when there was a shortage of such produce in the state, or the prices of such produce went beyond 25 per cent of the maximum price prevailing in the market within two years before the passing of the order by the state government. This was to undo the exemption given to contracting agencies under the central Contract Farming Act, 2020. Punjab had not provided for this in its amendments to the Central Act. The Rajasthan amendment also brought back contract farming dispute resolution to the APMC.

In sum, with its amendment bills, Punjab asserted its federal rights under the Constitution, ostensibly to protect farmer interests—though not as comprehensively as Rajasthan. However, the amendments suffered from the lacunae and problematic provisions discussed in this section. The result is likely to be ineffective protection of farmer interests, even if they withstand legal scrutiny by the courts. One might state even more strongly that Punjab's bills were bereft of any tangible benefits to the state's farmers, and did not do any service to the sustainability of its farm sector and farmers (Singh 2020c).

In November 2021, after the repeal of the Union Farm Acts in the same month, Punjab repealed the Contract Farming Act of 2013 (PVSS 2021a), undoing all amendments in the APMC Act from 2006 to 2017, and disallowed all private channels like private wholesale markets, direct purchase, or public private partnership in agricultural markets (PVSS 2021b).

## Rajasthan Contract Farming Act Amendments

Like the Punjab amendments, in the Rajasthan Contract Farming Act Amendment Bill, the MSP provision was brought in, which is applicable across all MSP crops, 'provided that no farming agreement for the sale or purchase of a crop shall be valid unless the price paid for such agricultural produce is equal to or greater than the prevailing MSP as announced by the central government for that crop' (GoR 2020). This is better than Punjab's amendment as it covers 23 crops, unlike the two (paddy and wheat) by the Punjab amendment. Any harassment of the farmer here is a punishable offence with not less than three years and up to seven years of imprisonment, or fine of not less than Rs 5,00,000, or both. But, in this Act, harassment of the farmer is defined differently as

> if a person, firm or company compels or exerts pressure on a farmer or any person associated with agriculture or agro produce to enter into a sale under contract of agricultural produce in his possession at a price below the MSP, and if a person, firm or company refuses to accept produce or take delivery of the goods under a farming agreement within a week from the date of intimation by the farmer of the produce being ready for delivery (GoR 2020).

This is an important provision to protect farmer interest in contract farming which Punjab failed to provide in its amendments but here too, this provision failed to recognise that horticultural produce which is highly perishable cannot wait for one week after intimation. This kind of poor provision showed that if all heads (central and state) were put together to frame such important legislations, the country would have designed a much better set of legislations.

Of course, this was a bad proposal per se, as we know contract price cannot be tied to any other price, especially state-declared prices, since contract prices should be discovered by the two parties.

However, the Rajasthan Act has a bad provision about contract farming where it includes sponsor undertaking farming deploying his/its manpower under the farming agreement, as stated earlier on p. 141.

The market committee was mandated to decide a dispute and to direct the sponsor to remove his/its manpower from the field/farm and for putting the farmer back to possession, it was entitled to take aid of the police. On such a request, the Superintendent of Police (SP) of the district was mandated to make the police help available within 24 hours on receipt of the request. This is an outright misperceived provision of the amended Act as a sponsor never cultivates farmer's field under contract farming arrangement since, as mentioned earlier, the farmer as a producer is central to this arrangement. It is unfortunate that the state confused contract farming with corporate farming, which it never is.

In both the amended Acts, like the Punjab amendments, the Rajasthan state government created its right to levy cess/cesses on notified- or contract-farmed agricultural produce bought, brought, or sold by a corporate or trader and/or on the electronic platform, as the case may be, for trade and commerce in a trade area, and this cess collection, like in the case of Punjab, would go into a fund to run the market committee and welfare of farmers or other purposes related to welfare and promotion of agriculture or agriculturists and development of market infrastructure. Rajasthan has also, like Punjab, brought back the power of civil court to dispute resolution as had existed under the APMC Act.

In sum, the Rajasthan government has, with these Bills, asserted its federal rights like Punjab and tried to protect farmer interests more comprehensively than Punjab, but the amendments suffered from above mentioned gaps which would make many provisions to protect farmer interest ineffective even if they pass legal examination by the courts. The Union government could have instead used Entry 7 of the Concurrent List to frame a law on contract farming, as it would have been about crop contract and not agricultural land contracts, which are not allowed under that entry since Entry 7 states: 'Contracts, including partnership, agency, contracts of carriage, and other special forms of contracts, but not including contracts relating to agricultural land'. (Constitution of India, Seventh Schedule). The above analysis shows that the Union government had constitutional options in the contract farming domain for enacting new laws but they were not exercised, and whatever was attempted under the repealed Contract Farming Act of 2020 was also poor in design and content.

## Note

1. The 'great Indian thali' refers to the Indian state offering an enabling environment to agribusiness corporations through various legal and policy changes.

## References

Banday, M. U. L., S. Chakraborty, P. D'Cruz, and E. Noronha. 2018. 'Abuse Faced by Child Labourers: Novel Territory in Workplace Bullying'. In P. D'Cruz, E. Noronha, A. Mendonca, and N. Mishr (eds), *Indian Perspectives on Workplace Bullying—A Decade of Insights*, pp. 173–204. Singapore: Springer Nature.

Cariappa, A. G. A., M. Sinha, S. Kharkwal, and A. Srinivas. 2003. 'Bearing Fruit or Falling Flat? The Story of Contract Farming in India'. *Agricultural Economics Research Review* 36(1): 21–24.

D'Cruz P., E. Noronha, M. U. L. Banday, and S. Chakraborty. 2021. 'Place matters: (Dis)embeddedness and child labourers' experiences of depersonalised bullying in Indian Bt cottonseed global production networks'. *Journal of Business Ethics*. Available at DoI: https://doi.org/10.1007/s10551-020-04676-1 (accessed August 2023).

Eaton, C. 1998. 'Contract farming: Structure and management in developing countries'. In D. Burch, G. Lawrence, R. E. Rickson, and J. Goss (eds), *Australian Food and Farming in a Globalised Economy: Recent Developments and Future Prospects*, Monash publications in Geography No. 50, pp. 127–144. Melbourne, Australia: Monash University.

FAO and IISD. 2018. *Model Agreement for Responsible Contract Farming, with Commentary*. Rome: FAO.

Gill, S. 2004. 'Small farmers and Markets' (a book review), *Economic and Political Weekly* 39(23): 2356–2358.

Glover, D. 1987. 'Increasing the Benefits to Smallholders from Contract Farming: Problems for Farmers' Organisations and Policy Makers'. *World Development* 15(4): 441–448.

GoP. 2020a. *The Farmers' Produce Trade and Commerce, (Promotion and Facilitation) (Special Provisions and Punjab Amendment) Bill, 2020, Punjab Vidhan Sabha Bill No. 32-PLA-2020*. Government of Punjab.

______. 2020b. *The Farmers (Empowerment and Protection) Agreement on Price Assurance and Farm Services (Special Provisions and Punjab Amendment) Bill, 2020, Punjab Vidhan Sabha Bill No. 33-PLA-2020*. Government of Punjab.

GoR. 2020. *The Farmers (Empowerment and Protection) Agreement on Price Assurance and Farm Services (Rajasthan Amendment) Bill, 2020, Bill No. 31 of 2020*. Government of Rajasthan.

GoTN. 2019. *Tamil Nadu Agricultural Produce and Livestock Contract Farming and Services (Promotion and Facilitation) Act, 2019*. Tamil Nadu Government Gazette Extraordinary, Government of Tamilnadu.

Haque, T. 2003. 'Land Reforms and Agricultural Development: Retrospect and Prospect'. In S. Pal et al. (eds), *Institutional Change in Indian Agriculture*, 267–284. New Delhi: NCAP.

IFPRI. 2005. 'High Value Agriculture and Vertical Co-ordination in India—Will the Smallholders Participate?', draft research report Washington: IFPRI.

Kaur, P., and N. Singla. 2018. Can Contract Farming Double Farmers' Income? *EPW* 53(51).

Khairnar, S., and V. Yeleti. 2005. 'Contract Farming in India: Impact and Implications'. In Ramesh Chand (ed), *India's Agricultural Challenges: Reflections on Policy, Technology and Other Issues*, 105–128. New Delhi: CENTAD.

Kumar, P. 2006. 'Contract Farming through Agribusiness Firms and State Corporation: A Case Study in Punjab'. *Economic and Political Weekly* 41(52): 5367–75.

Kumar, Shiv, Subhash Chandra, D. R. Singh, and Khyali Ram Chaudhary. 2013. 'Contractual Arrangements and Enforcement in India: The Case of Organic Basmati Paddy Farming'. *Indian Journal of Agricultural Economics* 68(3): 449–56.

Lawrence, G. 1999. 'Agro-food restructuring: A synthesis of recent Australian research'. *Rural Sociology* 64(2): 186–202.

Minten, B., L. Randrianarison, and J. F. M. Swinnen. 2006. 'Global supply chains, poverty and the environment: evidence from Madagascar'. In JFM Swinnen (ed.), *Global Supply Chains, Standards and the Poor*, 147–158. CAB International.

MoAFW. 2018. *Model Act [The State/UT Agricultural Produce and Livestock Contract Farming and Services (Promotion and Facilitation) Act, 2018]*, February. MoAFW, Department of Agriculture, Co-operation and Farmers' Welfare, Government of India.

______. 2020a. *The Farmers' Produce Trade and Commerce (Promotion and Facilitation) Bill*, No. 10 of 2020.

______. 2020b. *The Farmers (Empowerment and Protection) Agreement on Price Assurance and Farm Services Bill*, No. 11 of 2020. Ministry of Agriculture and Farmer Welfare, Government of India.

Opondo, M. 2000. 'The Socio-economic and Ecological Impacts of the Agro-industrial Food Chain on the Rural Economy in Kenya'. *Ambio* 29(1): 35–41.

Pultrone, C. 2012. 'An Overview of Contract Farming: Legal Issues and Challenges'. *Uniform Law Review* 17: 263–289.

PVSS. 2021a. *The Punjab Contract Farming (Repeal) Bill 2021, Bill No. 36-PLA-2021*. Punjab Vidhan Sabha Secretariat (PVSS), Chandigarh.

______. 2021b. *The Punjab Agricultural Produce Markets (Amendment) Bill 2021, Bill No. 35-PLA-2021*. Punjab Vidhan Sabha Secretariat (PVSS), Chandigarh.

Raynolds, L. T. 2000. 'Negotiating Contract Farming in the Dominican Republic'. *Human Organisation* 59(4): 441–451.

Rickson, R. E., and Burch, D. 1996. 'Globalised agriculture and agri-food restructuring in southeast Asia: The Thai experience'. In D. Burch, R. E. Rickson and G. Lawrence (eds), *Globalisation and Agri-Food Restructuring—Perspectives from the Australasia Region,* 323–344. Brookfield, USA: Avebury.

SC Committee. 2021. *Report of the Supreme Court Appointed Committee on Farm Laws*, March.

Shrimali, R. 2021. *Contract Farming, Capital and State: Corporatisation of Indian Agriculture*. Singapore: Palgrave Macmillan.

Singh, G., and S. R. Asokan. 2005. *Contract Farming in India—Text and Cases*. New Delhi: Oxford & IBH.

Singh, M. P. 2007. *Contract Farming and Emerging Agrarian Structure: The Case of Punjab*. PhD thesis. New Delhi: CSRD, JNU.

Singh, S. 2002. 'Contracting Out Solutions: Political Economy of Contract Farming in the Indian Punjab'. *World Development* 30(9): 1621–38.

______. 2004. 'Crisis and Diversification in Punjab Agriculture–Role of State and Agribusiness'. *Economic and Political Weekly* 39(52), December.

______. 2005. 'Role of the state in contract farming in Thailand: Experience and Lessons'. *ASEAN Economic Bulletin* 22(2): 217–228 (now called *Journal of Southeast Asian Economies* from 2013).

______. 2008a. 'Marketing channels and their implications for smallholder farmers in India'. In E. B. McCullough, P. L. Pingali, and K. G. Stamoulis (eds), *The Transformation of Agri-food Systems: Globalization, Supply Chains, and Smallholder Farmers*, 279–310. Rome and London: FAO and Earthscan Press.

______. 2008b. 'Gender and Child Labour in Cottonseed Production in India: A Case Study of Gujarat'. *Indian Journal of Labour Economics* 51(3): 445–458.

______. 2009. 'Supply Chains for High Value Crops: A Case Study of Mint in Punjab'. *Indian Journal of Agricultural Marketing* 23(1): 93–102.

______. 2011. 'Contract farming for sustainable agricultural development in India: A smallholder perspective', IGIDR Proceedings of Workshop on 'Policy Options and Investment Priorities for Accelerating Agricultural Productivity and Development in India' held at IIC, New Delhi, 10–11 November.

______. 2012. 'New Markets for Smallholders in India: Exclusion, Policy and Mechanisms'. *Economic and Political Weekly* 47(52): 95–105.

Singh, S. 2013. 'Regulating contract farming—Punjab way', 8 July, *The Tribune*, Op. ed. Agriculture, Chandigarh.

______. 2015. 'Reforming markets, lessons from Bihar', 6 February, *The Tribune*, Op. ed. Agriculture, Chandigarh.

______. 2017. '"White Gold" for Whom? A Study of Institutional Aspects of Work and Wages in Cotton GPNs in India'. In Ernesto Noronha and

Premila D'Cruz (eds), *Critical Perspectives on Work and Employment in Globalizing India*, 15–36. Singapore: Springer.

———. 2018. 'Reforming Agricultural Markets in India: A Tale of Two Model Acts'. *Economic and Political Weekly* 53(51).

———. 2020a. 'Separating grain from the chaff', 5 February, *The Pioneer*, p. 7.

———. 2020b. 'Amending Agri Market Law But Half-Heartedly', 17 February, *The Tribune*.

———. 2020c. 'A Bill to Corporatise Agriculture', 5 June, *Frontline*, pp. 97–98.

———. 2020d. 'Two Acts and a Half', 5 October, *Outlook*.

———. 2020e. 'Farm laws: Design leaves much to be desired', 13 October, *Ideas for India*.

———. 2020f. 'The (food)grain of Punjab's own farm Bills', 21 October, *Business Standard*.

———. 2020g. 'New investment needs incentives, not only ease of doing business', 21 October, *Times of India*.

———. 2020h. 'Farmers' Freedom at stake', 23 October, *Frontline*, pp. 27–31.

———. 2020i. 'Can Cong states' amended Acts help farmers?', 11 November, *The Hindu Business Line*, Op. Ed.

———. 2021a. 'Middleman's role', 1 January, *Frontline*.

———. 2021b. *Understanding Performance and Impact of Producer Companies: Case Studies across States and Promoters in India*, Final Report for MoAFW, CMA. Ahmedabad: IIM.

———. 2021c. 'Food Security and Markets: Understanding the Protests over India's Changing Social Contract with Farmers', *The Hindu Centre for Politics and Public Policy*, 15 March. Available at https://www.thehinducentre.com/the-arena/current-issues/article34060554.ece (accessed August 2023).

Singh, S. 2022. 'The (Repealed) Union Contract Farming Act, 2020: Corporatising Indian Agriculture'. *Economic and Political Weekly* 57(2).

Singh, S., and T. Singh. 2014. *Producer Companies in India: Organisation and Performance*. New Delhi: Allied Publishers.

Sinha, S. 2020. 'The agrarian crisis in Punjab and the making of the anti-farm law protests', 4 December, *The India Forum*.

Swain, B. B. 2011. 'Contract farming in Andhra Pradesh: A case of rice seed and gherkin cultivation'. *Economic and Political Weekly* 46(42): 60–68.

six

# The MSP Question

In 2020–21, the various farmer unions protesting against the three Union Farm Laws (now repealed) were demanding MSP (Minimum Support Price) as a legal right for all crops. The largest grouping of the unions, the Samyukta Kisan Morcha (SKM) which was spearheading the protests wanted it to be made into a legal right for farmers for all crops, based on the Swaminathan Commission formula of comprehensive cost plus 50 per cent margin over it. The right-wing Bharatiya Kisan Sangh (BKS) which had not fully opposed the new Acts demanded a *laabhkari* (remunerative) MSP. The Rashtriya Kisan Manch (RKM) which even formally wrote to the government asking for some specific amendments in the new Acts and not their total repeal, demanded a guaranteed MSP as the floor price for contract-farmed produce and having it written in the Contract Farming Act, besides MSP being made a legal right for all farmers for all crops/produces.

Many academic scholars also justify the demand for legal MSP due to the growing global trends in corporate control of agriculture and the low bargaining power of the Indian small farmers, besides the fact that the Indian state may withdraw from farm produce market due to its neoliberal policies, which have led to farmers not getting MSP for their produce in most crops and places (Singh and Bhogal 2021).

The limitation of MSP mechanism as operated now becomes evident from an estimation carried out by Balaji et al. (2017), wherein it is shown that in the case of gram, in order to double farmer incomes by 2022 in the states of Madhya Pradesh, Maharashtra, and Rajasthan, the farm harvest prices needed to increase by Rs 200 to Rs 600 per quintal which would have given higher per hectare income of the order of Rs 1000 to Rs 4000. On the other hand, in the case of arhar, an MSP increase of Rs 200 to Rs 600 across the states would have doubled the real farmer income though this would have been lower, that is, Rs 500 to Rs 3000 per ha., than the farmer incomes at the time. This assumed 10 per cent increase over the existing MSP.

A recent study shows that in case of cotton in one district of Telangana, the percentage of produce procured by CCI (Cotton Corporation of India) ranged from 0.6 per cent to as high as 93.85 per cent across years, averaging 28.9 per cent of total produce, but only 66 per cent of cotton in 2019–20 was sold at MSP and rest below MSP, wherein 50 per cent of farmers were either leased or tenant farmers with average holding of all farmers being 3.5 acres. The public sales were low due to poor procurement support and delay in payments (Abhilasha and Janaiah 2021).

Minimum Support Price has a role in production enhancement, and therefore, in ensuring food security both in terms of physical availability as well as access to food through better and more assured farmer incomes. It can thus play a role in farmer income stabilisation as well as income enhancement. The MSP also has a role in crop diversification by incentivising certain crops against others, so far as protection from price risk for the farmer from the farmer-risk perspective is concerned. However, the major question in this domain is: Under what conditions should MSP be offered and how should MSP be determined? Further, it necessarily involves not just announcing MSPs for different crops, but also having in place certain public procurement at MSP or other mechanisms to reduce farmers' market risk. In fact, the need for MSP in a developing country like India which has non-available, or imperfect, inefficient markets, and poor price discovery also come from the fact that once a farmer takes the produce to a mandi, it is not possible to take it back especially when long distances are involved, which raises farmer transaction cost, or when the farmer is unable to wait for a better or more appropriate price for the produce. In fact, it can be said that a farmer taking her crop produce to the mandi is like taking a dead body to the mortuary or a cremation ground, which cannot be brought back or held back for long.

The major issues in the way the MSP system works presently in India include: procurement only for two to three crops, procurement only in some states, delayed procurement as state agencies enter the markets late, location of procurement centres which are not accessible for all farmers, quantitative restrictions in some states in terms of how much produce can be sold to the procurement agencies at MSP, fair and average quality, paper work, and delayed payment. Another issue that plagues the MSP system is: banks recover their loans from MSP sales proceeds of the crops sold to public agencies like FCI (Food Corporation of India), which is done from farmer bank accounts into which money goes. Farmers do not get a control over these sales proceeds amounts and often get little money in hand for other needs. Therefore, they do not want to sell to government agencies even at MSP.

Further, despite the existence of MSP-based procurement system for the last five decades for 23 crops for which MSP is announced during a year, APMC mandi sales still account for a very small proportion of the total marketed surplus of these crops produce, ranging from 10–64 per cent with the rest of the produce being sold outside the APMC mandi system. It is important to recall that MSP-based procurement happens only in APMC mandi yards and sub-yards. Most of the produce is sold to private traders (60–80 per cent), except paddy and wheat (40 per cent and 30 per cent of the season, respectively), and only less than 20 per cent is sold to the cooperative channel in wheat and paddy. It is interesting to note that in Kharif, only 4 per cent (sugarcane) to 59 per cent (soyabean) farmers across crops sold through the APMC market, and only in paddy and sugarcane, a significant proportion (17 per cent and 50 per cent) was sold through the cooperative or the government agency. The APMC mandi sales for Rabi ranged from 2 per cent in sugarcane to 64 per cent in gram, and 6 per cent and 57 per cent through the cooperative and the government channels for sugarcane and paddy, respectively. Interestingly, in maize and wheat, there was significant presence of the cooperative and the government channel during Rabi season (15 per cent and 19 per cent). Farmers had sold mostly sugarcane, paddy, and cotton to procurement agencies in Kharif season, and sugarcane, jowar, barley, and paddy besides cotton, in Rabi season. The awareness of MSP was very low (<20 per cent) across the crops other than sugarcane, paddy, coconut, wheat, cotton, and jowar (from 20 per cent to 45 per cent across crops), and the procurement agency awareness even lower than this (<10 and <15 per cent in Kharif and Rabi seasons). Surprisingly, in crops like arhar, cotton, soyabean, jowar, and mung in Kharif, and cotton and arhar in Rabi, a significant proportion of farmers reported receiving better market price than MSP, and therefore, had not sold to the government agency at MSP (Mukesh and Srivastava 2019).

The NSO Survey for 2012–13 showed that only 6 per cent paddy and wheat farmers sold at MSP; even if paddy and wheat sales are considered separately, only 14 per cent and 16 per cent sold paddy and wheat at MSP, respectively. In the case of paddy only 43 per cent of those who grew it, sold it, and further only 13.4 per cent of them sold at MSP. In the case of wheat, 36.9 per cent growers sold it and only 16.2 per cent of them sold it at MSP. Besides this, there is the question of who gets access to MSP-based sale of produce and therefore, benefits from it. It is only large farmers or others who have access to this price protection–based sale channel. It is interesting to find that whereas 20.29 per cent of those operating more than 4 ha. sold at MSP, of the marginal, small, and semi-medium categories which account for more than 90 per cent of farming households and 50 per cent of land, only 4.65 per cent sold at MSP. Another important question in this domain is, is it the number of farmers who sold at MSP or the volume sold at MSP? For example, only 6 per cent farmers may sell at MSP but given that they are large land operators, the quantity sold at MSP would be disproportionately higher. In the case of Odisha, the Commission for Agricultural Costs and Prices (CACP) in its report had highlighted that more than 80 per cent paddy procured at MSP in the state came from large, medium, and semi-medium farmers, which shows that MSP does not reach small and marginal farmers. In 2016–17, paddy procured by the government agencies at MSP was 27.9 per cent of production and 34 per cent of marketed surplus, which had increased from 22.9 per cent and 30.7 per cent respectively in 2002–03. It was also found that in the 2020 paddy season, 83 per cent in Gujarat, 63 per cent in Karnataka, 60 per cent in Telangana, and of the total market arrivals in mandis in UP, 47 per cent was sold below MSP with the overall percentage being 77 per cent.

Another argument often made is that MSP benefits farmers only in some states like Punjab and Haryana. The empirical facts show that majority of the procurement may be taking place in these states in the case of wheat and paddy, but there are many other states and their farmers like Madhya Pradesh or Chhattisgarh which also benefit from MSP-based procurement because geography of procurement is changing over time due to the decentralised procurement system. There are 17 states today which practise decentralised procurement especially in eastern central and south India, and their share has increased from 30.6 per cent in 2010–11 to 54.3 per cent in 2015–16 Kharif marketing season. This was just 10 per cent of paddy and wheat before 2000. In fact, Odisha and Chhattisgarh accounted for 10 per cent each of paddy procurement and Madhya Pradesh alone accounted for 20 per cent of wheat procurement thus overtaking Punjab. Further, 45 per cent of the sellers at MSP was small or marginal farmers. The CACP report of Kharif 2015–16 for paddy highlights that for Punjab which has 12.8 per cent share in marketed surplus of paddy, its procurement share was 25.7 per cent. Similarly, Haryana with marketed surplus share of 4.4 per cent had 7.4 per cent of procurement. Similarly, Chhattisgarh with a marketed surplus share of 6.6 per cent had a procurement share of 11.4 per cent. Odisha was no different with a share of 5.9 per cent and 8.9 per cent respectively as was the case with AP and Telangana together accounting for 12 per cent of marketed surplus but 21.5 per cent of procurement. On the other hand, there are states which produce much higher shares and have higher marketed surpluses but do not benefit from public procurement at MSP. For example, Uttar Pradesh had a market surplus share of 12.9 per cent but its share in procurement was 5.8 per cent. Similarly West Bengal had shares of 12.1 per cent and 5 per cent, respectively. Bihar with a marketed surplus of 5.9 per cent had a procurement share of 3.9 per cent. Independent studies show that only 16 per cent of all households selling at MSP in case of paddy were in Punjab and Haryana, with 11 per cent being in Odisha and 33 per cent in Chhattisgarh. In case of wheat, Punjab and

Haryana had 40 per cent of all households selling at MSP, and in Madhya Pradesh alone 33 per cent of households were selling at MSP. Further, 70 per cent of farmers selling paddy at MSP were marginal or small and it was 56 per cent in wheat. In fact, in Punjab which has larger land holdings, 34 per cent of all farming households who are marginal or small accounted for 38 per cent of those who sold paddy at MSP. In case of Haryana, small and marginal farmers accounted for 58 per cent for those selling at MSP. Farmers selling at MSP realised 13 per cent higher price in paddy and 6 per cent in wheat (Gupta et al. 2020). There is no doubt that the public procurement system of wheat and paddy at MSP has led to these states' over dependence on MSP-based systems. For example, 90 per cent of the paddy was procured by state agencies at MSP in Punjab during the 2019–20 Kharif season followed by 88 per cent in Haryana and 80 per cent in Telangana (CACP 2021). Similarly, in the 2020–21 season, 99.5 per cent of wheat arrivals in Punjab were procured and 97 per cent farmers received MSP for wheat even when it was in the midst of the Covid-19 pandemic situation.

The farmers' concern for the state moving away from MSP-based procurement system comes from not just the recently repealed Farm Acts but also other official documents like the Shanta Kumar Committee Report, which recommended the end of open-ended procurement by FCI and CACP, suggesting shifting procurement to states other than Punjab and Haryana. Besides, there was the NITI report of 2018 (NITI 2018) which recommended a minimum reserve price (MRP) which could be the starting point for auctions at mandis, instead of MSP. The CACP report of 2020–21 (CACP 2021) recommended review of open-ended procurement for Punjab and Haryana due to the ground water depletion these crops cause, and in case of other states, which offer bonus over and above the MSP.

In fact, the SC Committee also found MSP-based procurement unsustainable and recommended a cap on wheat and paddy procurement instead of open-ended procurement, and proposed adopting the NAFED approach of buying certain percentage of a crop (upto 25 per cent of production) to stabilise open market prices around MSP, and recommended leaving procurement to states which can legalise it, if so desired by them, with the Union government only providing allocation of funds for such state-level procurement operation (SC Committee 2021). Therefore, it absolved the Union government of any obligations to ensure MSP to farmers even on crops which it announces MSPs for.

It is argued that if a mandatory MSP has to be assured for all 23 crops for which MSPs are declared then it would cost Rs 7.5 lakh crore, and if for all crops which number 36, then it may amount to Rs 17 lakh crore for procurement, which is seen as unaffordable by the government. But these numbers need to be seen more carefully since, of today, the Government of India declares MSP for 23 crops—seven cereals (rice, wheat, maize, bajra, sorghum, ragi, and barley); five pulses (tuvar, moong, chana, urad, and masoor); seven oilseeds (soyabean, groundnut, green seed mustard, sesamum, safflower, sunflower, and Niger seed) and four commercial crops (sugarcane, cotton, jute, and copra). However, only a few of these crops, mainly wheat and rice are procured to feed the public distribution system (PDS). The PDS prices of wheat and rice are subsidised up to 90 per cent of their economic cost to the government. In 2020–21, the food subsidy bill was around 30 per cent of the net tax revenue of the Union government. It was also argued that if MSP was made mandatory for all buyers of agricultural produce for 23 crops, it is possible that private buyers would not buy if the MSP was not affordable for them. In that case, the government would have to become the buyer of last resort and if the government failed to buy, then farmers would be left high and dry with no buyer for their produce, making them worse off. It was claimed that even after procuring more than 50 per cent of the marketed surplus of rice and wheat, the market prices of these produces remained below MSP in several states. For example, in November 2020 market prices of paddy in Chhattisgarh were Rs 300 per quintal lower than its MSP and the gap was Rs 102 per quintal in Uttar Pradesh, and there were many states like Bihar, Jharkhand, and Assam in a similar situation. Similarly, in case of wheat, the crops sold at below MSP in two largest wheat producer states of UP and MP. Therefore, it was argued that even if after buying more than 50 per cent of the marketed surplus by the state, the prices ruled below MSP, it was unrealistic to expect that MSP-based public procurement can assure that all farmers get MSP.

Further it is argued that even if 10 per cent of the production of remaining crops, excluding sugarcane, is procured at MSP, it will cost the government Rs 5.4 lakh crore annually. This cost includes economic cost of operation of buying agencies that are generally about 30 per cent higher than MSP and as high as 40 per cent in case of rice and wheat. Another question asked in this context of legalisation of MSP for 23 crops is that why not offer the same to the farmers of other agricultural produce like milk, which has even higher value than cereal crops of wheat and paddy and sugarcane combined. Even the mechanism of deficiency price payment (DPP), under which the government need not buy farmers' produce to ensure access to MSP but only needs to pay the difference between MSP and price realised by the farmer seller, is dismissed arguing that this mechanism was tried in Madhya Pradesh across eight crops of pulses and oilseeds in 2017 but had to be given up due to the traders gaming it and widening the gap between market price and MSP and benefitting massively from the scheme, instead of farmers getting the benefit. Therefore, those against the idea of legalisation of MSP suggest direct transfer of cash payments to the farmers based on area owned or operated and argue that legalisation of MSP would be market distorting (Gulati and Saini 2020).

The above argument needs to be questioned on many counts. *First*, it is wrong to assume that government will have to buy all of the farmers' produce. The figures cited above as procurement cost for the government are based on the entire value of total output of these crops and therefore, Rs 17 lakh crore becomes almost 50 per cent of the annual budget of Government of India for 2021–22. It is important to exclude the retained output at the farmer level for various purposes including own consumption. For example, in 2019–20, the total value of 23 crop output was estimated to be Rs 10.8 lakh crore. Out of this, if on an average, 25 per cent is retained for home consumption and other uses, then this amount comes down to Rs 8 lakh crore. *Second*, if government purchases up to a certain proportion of the total market surplus, say 20–30 per cent, to play its market intervention role, then this expenditure will further come down. In 2020–21, the CCI bought only 25 per cent of the total market arrivals of cotton and this led to the market prices going up beyond MSP. Further, out of Rs 8 lakh crore, if sugarcane purchases are excluded as they are made by the sugar mills at FRP (Fair and Remunerative Price) or SAP (State Advised Price), then the total expenditure comes down further and one-third of the total market arrivals will amount to only Rs 3 lakh crore. It is also important to recognise that when the government will buy farm produce from farmers at MSP, it is not going to buy waste but valuable food and fibre material, which will realise its value in the market though there may be some losses in that further sale. Additionally, when India is spending valuable foreign exchange on import of pulses and oilseeds then it is important that the same money is used for encouraging domestic production with an assured MSP, which can also help crop diversification to enhance farmer income and save precious natural resources. Another example of government intervention leading to the market prices becoming as good as MSP is borne out by Karnataka's experience of arhar dal wherein only purchase of 2.5 lakh tonnes out of 14 lakh tonnes under Market Intervention Scheme (MIS) stabilised the market prices. Similarly, in cotton in Punjab, only 35 per cent of the purchases of total arrivals by CCI led to market prices going above MSP.

So far as the rationale for MSP as a legal right is concerned, the farmers' unions argued that if there could be principle of one nation–one market, then why not one nation–one price. They also argued that if there could be right to food or minimum wages in various occupation then why not right to minimum price for the farmer produce. They maintained that cheap food causes rural poverty as farmers and farm workers cannot earn enough, and therefore, those who can afford to pay higher for food should pay, and everybody need not be provided subsidised or cheap food. They also found more merit in price protection being more effective and desirable for farmer incomes as it would benefit all cultivators and farmers, unlike cash payments which mostly target landowners and exclude off-farm and allied activity farmers dealing with milk, fish, and meat. In this regard, a private member Bill was introduced in Parliament in 2017–18, which provided for a remunerative MSP as C2[1] + 50 per cent for every farmer as a right and for all crops and produce in all markets and channels. It also suggested MSP as floor auction price in APMC mandis or any other purchase location and no purchases being allowed below such MSP. It also provided for a legal status to the central- and state-level CACPs, which should be headed by a farmer each, and whose recommendations should be mandatory for government so far as guaranteed remunerative MSP (GRMSP) and regulation of input cost to manage such an MSP are concerned.

It is also interesting to note that the legalisation of MSP as an idea did originate in many government documents. For example, the CACP (2018) report of Kharif 2017–18 has this to say, 'to instil confidence among farmers for procurement of their produce, a legislation conferring on farmers "The Right to sell at MSP" may be brought out'. Similarly, a NITI Aayog report (NITI 2018) which examined the Minimum Reserved Price (MRP) by an expert group recommended 'replacing MSP with MRP which could be the starting point for auctions at mandis'. It further suggested 'replacing CACP by an Agricultural tribunal as per article 323(b) of the Constitution'. Even the Dalwai Committee on Doubling of Farmers' Income also recommended MRP at A2 + FL + 50 per cent as the floor price for any purchases by any buyer.[2] The above shows that the cat among the pigeons was let loose by the government committees and reports, and not just farmer unions.

Here it is important to examine limited state-level experience of making MSP legal to protect farmer interest. In Madhya Pradesh, in the APMC Act, it is stated that no sale of a crop produce should take place below MSP declared by the state government for the crop in question, and no bid should be permitted to start below such MSP in APMC auction in the state's mandis. The Madhya Pradesh APMC Act states:

> provided that, in the market yard, the price for such notified agricultural produce of which support price has been declared by the State Government shall not be settled below the price so declared and no bid shall be permitted to start, in the market yard below the rate so fixed (MPSAMB 2005: 37).

This provision has been a part of state APMC Act since 1986 but the state has never declared its own MSP for any crop so far and therefore, the question of implementation of this measure did not arise. Similarly, Maharashtra had amended its APMC Act in 2018 making all purchases in APMC mandis at least at prices which are on par with MSP. The traders in the mandis went on strike and within a week, the state had to withdraw the said amendment. The above shows that it is not desirable to adopt such measures of farmer interest protection without considering the implications of such measures for the open market and all the stakeholders involved. Chand (2020) also argued that the MSP was being unnecessarily linked with new Acts as MSP and procurement are purely administrative decisions, and some states like Bihar and Kerala have been procuring at MSP without having APMC structure or regulation. He cites the cases of the Maharashtra APMC Act amendment of 2018 and the Fair and Remunerative Price (FRP) for sugarcane, which did not go down well as a legal or mandatory price for farm produce by the private buyers, and this model cannot be sustainable.

Even if the argument of the farmer unions for the right to MSP as a legal measure is accepted from the rights perspective, it is important to apply the rights framework in an appropriate manner. Here the examples of MGNREGA (Mahatma Gandhi National Rural Employment Guarantee Act) and Food Security Act can help as both these legal rights to the intended stakeholders make it mandatory for the state to deliver this mandate, and do not involve the private sector in it even though private sector also provides employment to the people and also sells food products to consumers. Therefore, seen in this light, the legal right to MSP should only mandate the Government of India, which declares MSP for various crops, to be responsible for delivering this right and not tie the private sector into it since the latter never promised any minimum price to farmers, and they go by demand-and-supply dynamics to discover farmer-level purchase price. Also, in a capitalist market system, it is not desirable to expect the state to impose price controls on buyers. It is also at cross purposes with the government direction of opening-up the agricultural market to bring new channels and private buyers into the market as legal MSP would discourage them.

The government can easily implement a legal guarantee to MSP by using various existing mechanisms such as public procurement, DPP, and MIS. There are various innovations in MSP-based procurement and delivery system like decentralised procurement which can be brought in. Further, warehouse receipt system–based credit to farmers and staggered purchase and storage being incentivised can also help prevent distress sale at harvest. Further changing the crop focus of MSP-based procurement is much needed as are local institutions for their involvement in public procurement as in Odisha, Kerala, and Bihar. The MSP is a double-edged weapon, and can cut both ways if not used smartly, and therefore it is also important to re-examine the purpose of MSP in terms of whether it is for farmer income enhancement or income stabilisation.

## Notes

1. C2 stands for comprehensive cost of production, which includes all paid out and imputed costs of production, including rent for owned land.
2. FL stands for family labour; A2 is cost of production which includes only paid out costs, not all costs.

## References

Abhilasha, A., and A. Janaiah. 2021. 'Marketing and Procurement of Cotton: Farmers' Experiences in Adilabad District of Telangana'. *Economic and Political Weekly* 46(49): 24–27.

Balaji, S. J., P. Kishore, R. Saxena, N. P. Singh, and D. Franco. 2017. 'Technology-Policy Tradeoff in Doubling Farmers' Income: A Case Study on Pulses'. *Agricultural Economics Research Review* 30: 117–126.

CACP. 2018. *Price Policy for Kharif Crops: The Marketing Season 2018–19*, March. New Delhi: Department of Agriculture, Cooperation and Farmers Welfare, Ministry of Agriculture and Farmers Welfare, Government of India.

CACP. 2021. *Price Policy for Kharif Crops: The Marketing Season 2021–22*, March. New Delhi: Department of Agriculture, Cooperation and Farmers Welfare Ministry of Agriculture and Farmers Welfare, Government of India, Krishi Bhawan.

Chand, R. 2020. *New Farm Acts: Understanding the Implications*. New Delhi: National Institution for Transforming India (NITI), GoI, November.

Gulati, A., and S. Saini. 2020. 'Supporting Agriculture the Smart Way', December, *Financial Express*.

Gupta, P., R. Khera, and S. Narayanan. 2020. 'MSP–The Factoids versus the Facts', 19 December, *The Hindu*.

MPSAMB. 2005. *M P Krish Upaj Mandi Adhiniyam*, 1972 (MP Act No. 24 of 1973), up to date amended Act. Bhopal: MPSAMB.

Mukesh and N. Srivastava. 2019. 'Data Driven Road Map for Doubling Income for Farmers of India'. *Statistics and Applications* 17(1): 235–259.

NITI. 2018. *Strategy for India @75*, November. New Delhi: NITI Aayog.

SC Committee. 2021. *Report of the Supreme Court Appointed Committee on Farm Laws*, March.

Singh, P., and S. Bhogal. 2021. 'Interrogating the MSP Regime: Farm Laws and Agrarian Future in India'. *Millennial Asia* 12(3): 332–349.

# seven

# Conclusions

A very robust econometric analysis of the role of agricultural market regulation, as implemented through the APMC (Agricultural Produce Market Committee) Acts in agricultural and rural growth, for the period 1970–2008, revealed that APMC Acts significantly promoted not only agricultural growth but also use and adoption of agricultural technology. It argued that given this evidence, a policy to remove market regulation rather than bringing in more effective ones would fail to draw investments or improve agricultural growth (Purohit et al. 2017).

If the inter-state trade is a limiting factor in free and efficient operation of agricultural produce markets, then the Union government can very well legislate only on inter-state trade under Entry 42 of the Union List. It is important to remember that the trade transaction between an APMC-licensed trader and an outside trader who buys from this trader is not in the purview of APMC, as the APMC Act only deals with farmer-level sale of produce (first transaction between farmer and buyer directly or through commission agents), not secondary or tertiary transactions after that.

On the other hand, even contract farming can be legislated under Entry 7 of the Concurrent List as it is completely about contracts, and does not involve agricultural land. As we have discussed, contract farming is more about crop contract rather than land contract.

However, the larger questions about the repealed Acts were: Can one size fit all in a country like India where there is so much diversity in the level and nature of market structure and institutions? For example, Punjab may be ready for contract farming or direct purchase, but not Odisha. Similarly, some states have functional APMC infrastructure while others have none, yet others may have dismantled it like Bihar with a single stroke of a pen in 2006. Further, the new Acts brought a new phenomenon of moving from deregulation to re-regulation in some states like Bihar or even Kerala, which had no APMC Act ever.

Further, it is one thing to think of one law for the entire country for agricultural trading (though first transaction at the farmer level cannot be called trading, especially when it involves contract farming and therefore, it is still part of agricultural marketing), but another to see who would regulate such transactions when they are outside the domain of APMCs which are being restricted to their market yards and sub-yards only.

As mentioned earlier while examining the rationale for the new Act, the Model APMC Act, 2003 and the Model APLM [Agricultural Produce and Livestock Marketing (Promotion and Facilitation)] Act of 2017 provide for single licence within the state. The e-NAM (e-National Agriculture Market) provides for any trader from anywhere bidding for the produce in a local APMC mandi. Further, the 2003 Model APMC Act, the 2017 Model APLM Act, and the 2018 Model Contract Farming and Services Act allow direct purchase from farmers, private wholesale markets, and contract farming, and any place can be designated as a market yard. Therefore, there was no need to tamper with the APMC Act and the state's autonomy in a federal framework (except the inter-state trade which could have been legislated under the Union List).

However, some aspects of the state-level amendments and farmer demands which need to be questioned include: one, that traditional intermediaries are not bad! Arthiyas or CAs (commission agents) were being called 'service providers'! Why defend them? Rather, they should have been removed like in Madhya Pradesh during the 1980s. Even if they were allowed to operate in APMC mandis, they should not have been allowed to interlock credit with farm produce sales, and their commissions which were earlier driven by state purchases should have been rationalised.

Another bad proposal was to link contract price to MSP (Minimum Support Price). Haryana had tried it in the APMC Act, 2003. But, what about crops which do not have MSP? Also, if APMC prices are not discovered efficiently why should they drive other channel prices? To reiterate, it is also important to remember that contract farming is not about higher prices alone. The benefits can also include better quality produce, higher yields, new market access, lower costs, or other support like credit, insurance, and the like.

Finally, it is important not to mix policy and regulation. The present set of arguments in favour of the repealed Acts brought in MSP and procurement, or FPOs (Farmer Producer Organisations), or credit all of which were policy measures for improving agricultural and farmer performance. Regulation was intended to protect interest of weaker parties and provide a clear and fair framework for working together in markets as buyers and sellers. It should have done that and not attempted to interfere in anything which fell under the domain of policy. Also, the role and the goodness of regulatory measures should be assessed per se and that is what this book has attempted to do. There can be many policy measures to improve markets for agricultural produce and farmer incomes, but that is a separate question and a different domain.

The larger questions about agricultural market regulation and development like—Do we need more mandis or more deregulation? Would only more mandis do or do we need more functional and effective mandis?—still remain despite the repeal of the 2020 Acts. However, it needs to be recognised that Indian agricultural produce markets are decentralised and dynamic, and defy one-size-fit-all solutions as seen in the past. One agrees that the APMCs in some states are inefficient and ridden with corruption and malpractices, but is moving away from APMCs all together the solution? Should we throw away the baby along with the bath water, or should we reform them as they are the last resort for millions of marginal and small farmers who would never be attractive to corporate buyers, whether individually or collectively through FPOs? The decision to do away with the APMC regime on grounds of inefficiency and monopsony is similar to the argument against practising democracy. Should we give up democracy or federalism because it is not working smoothly? If self-reliance is the purpose of these reforms, should it be achieved through corporates or through people's agencies like APMCs and FPOs? Given the interlocking of credit and produce markets in many states, the solutions seem to lie outside the mandi. Therefore, what is needed is to reach institutional credit for small farmers before they can exercise choice in existing markets or new markets and market channels.

It is argued by the supporters of the repealed Farm Acts that the consultation process had been going on since 2001, but what was reported there was the expert committee reports, task force, and Model Acts but no public consultations. On the other hand, the Seed Bill and the Pesticides Bill, which are much less significant than the Agricultural Market Acts have been under public discussion and debate for the last 20 and 15 years, respectively, including some parliamentary committees examining them, unlike the Farm Acts.

It is important to realise that the farm prices in India demand multiple interventions in various markets like credit, labour, input, land, and produce because of the interlocked functioning of these markets. Without addressing the unequal balance of power in these markets, a fundamentalist notion of reform implying less state intervention can only amount to giving farmers more 'freedom to be exploited'. The freedom of choice for the weak and excluded lies in the direction of state support as they suffered for centuries within exploitative social structure, excluding them from land ownership and forcing them into relationships of profound inequality and discrimination (Shah 2021).

Finally, it is important to realise that whatever expansion contract farming and direct purchase may witness, India's large mass of marginal and small farmers would need public markets to be reformed and private markets set up, as they are the last resort for a large majority of them. These markets need to be reformed in terms of free licensing for better competition, e-payment of market fee, ensuring open auction, better facilities, representation of producer companies in APLM management, and even denotification of CAs/arthiyas as Madhya Pradesh did in 1985 though it is not widely known and discussed even today. The reform of APLM markets is important as they serve as competitors to contract farming and 'direct' purchase practised by food supermarkets and other buyers, and even proposed private wholesale markets, and can help improve the terms offered by food supermarkets to growers as contract/direct prices are unfortunately benchmarked to APLM prices, and the Act also takes this route to contract prices by linking them to MSP.

Better and more effective regulation is the first step to protect farmer interests and to ensure that they benefit from CF (contract farming) engagement. Further, since many Indian farmers are marginal or small, they cannot deal with large buyers on their own, even if they are brought under CF by some companies. Therefore, group contracts should be encouraged by policy incentives to make the mechanism inclusive and effective for farmers. The government can facilitate such contracts through credit and extension like in Thailand (Singh 2005a, 2005b). Also, India now has thousands of Farmer Producer Companies (FPCs), which are business-like entities representing farmers. They can play a role in making CF deliver the objectives of farmer income enhancement by facilitating CF with smallholders, and also undertaking CF on their own (Singh 2021; Singh and Singh 2014). They should have been given more careful and detailed treatment in the repealed Acts.

Given the experience of the impacts of contract farming on natural resources in Punjab (Singh, M. P. 2007), there is also a need to provide for ecological concerns in contract farming regulation. This can be done by way of land-use planning based on soil depth, soil quality, land slope, and suitable water availability. It is also important to understand previous land use and make it mandatory to follow appropriate crop rotations, if necessary (Singh 2011).

There is no doubt that the two Union Acts were poorly designed as regulatory mechanisms. The aspects of farmer empowerment and protection mentioned in the title of the Contract Farming Act had been neglected in its contents. The APMC mandi bypass Act also had 'promotion and facilitation' in its title, and not regulation (MoAFW 2020). Finally, the proof of any law is in its implementation, but as far as farmer interest protection is concerned, these Acts left much to be desired in their basic design.

The system of arthiyas in Punjab should be abolished by APMC Act amendment, with their place being taken by FPOs such as Primary Agricultural Credit Societies (PACS), other cooperatives, or producer companies, as is the case in states like Bihar, Madhya Pradesh, and even Uttar Pradesh now, where Food Corporation of India (FCI) and state agencies procure from village and local level without going to APMC mandis. Only then can small and marginal farmers hope to exercise choice of channels to benefit from direct purchase in trade area or from competition in the market. Of course, this requires better access to institutional credit for small and marginal farmers to get them out of the interlocking of credit and produce markets practised by the CAs in states like Punjab and Haryana.

It is difficult to police contracts due to the multiple variables involved in a farming contract like output price, input prices and supply, payments, and quality standards (Glover 1987; Wolf et al. 2001). Therefore, if the firm really wants to manipulate/sabotage a contract, there are a dozen ways to do it. A government cannot really do much to police a contract, and it should not impose contract on an unwilling firm or in an inappropriate situation. Further, the state/government may not always stand by the small growers due to the pressure from the agribusiness interests and may suffer from the conflicting objectives of its various agencies. Since policy interventions cannot really change the outcome of a fundamentally unworkable situation and the relevance of CF for small farmer development, it is better to have more realistic expectations about the intervention effect and define an appropriate niche for smallholder CF in terms of crops and markets. It is better to plan carefully *ex ante* for contract farming based on earlier experiences elsewhere (Glover 1987). But, still, the state/government can play both regulatory and enabling/developmental role in CF.

Legal protection to contract growers as a group must be considered to protect their interest. There are cases of legal protection given to subcontracting industries in Japan in their relations with large firms. These laws specify the duties (to have a written and clear terms contract with the subcontractor) and forbidden acts for the large parent firm. The latter include refusal to receive delivery of commissioned goods, delaying the payment beyond agreed period, discounting of payment, returning commissioned goods without good reason, forced price reduction, compulsory purchase by subcontractors of parental firm's products, and forcing subcontractors to pay in advance for materials supplied by the parent firm. These provisions were monitored by the Fair Trade Commission. Interestingly, most of the violations by parent firms were on the written form and clear terms of the contracts (Sako 1992). If CF is about flexible production systems becoming relevant to the farm production sector, then it is only logical to extend such legal provisions with necessary modifications to farming contracts. In farming sector per se, there is the Model Producer Protection Act, 2000 of Iowa State in the USA which requires contracts to be in plain language and disclose material risks. It provides a three days' cancellation period for the producer to review and discuss production contracts with their advisors. It also provides for producers to be first priority lien for payments due under a contract in case of contracting company bankruptcy. Besides, it protects against undue cancellation of contracts by companies and prohibits 'tournaments' (contracts where compensation to grower is determined by his performance relative to others) (ILSR n.d.).

Contracts need to be transparent with frequent and independent scrutiny so that they remain competitive both with similar contracts and with open market transactions. This can come only from a strong legal, regulatory, and institutional framework with clear rights and remedies though contracts are incomplete by nature. Wide publicity of contract terms can help to stimulate competition.

For CF to succeed, both regulation and policy are needed, and one cannot do the job of another. Contract should be fair to both the parties and enforcement mechanism should be clear and credible. There should be promotion of grades and quality standards among growers besides credit support and extension provision by public agencies, the state should not promote CF in non-viable situations or intervene too much, and incentives should be time-bound and short-term. Most importantly, competition in CF among buyers is a must to give choices to farmers to receive competitively discovered prices and other benefits (Chamber 2015). Many times, government projects in the contract crop can drive away private agencies from CF (Lambrecht and Ragasa 2018).

The experience of CF across the globe suggests that it is not the contract per se which is harmful as a system, but how it is practised in a given context. If there are enough mechanisms like group contracts, producer companies/associations, NGOs, and regulation of contracts, to monitor and use the contracts for facilitating development of smallholders, it can certainly lead to a betterment of all the parties involved, especially small and marginal farmers. In the emerging environment of 'triple bottom line' of people, planet, and profits, corporate agencies need to incorporate the 'people' and 'planet' concerns into their strategies and actions so that sustainability of both business as well as smallholders is achieved and sustained.

## References

Asokan, S. R., and G. Singh. 2006. *Contract Farming of Medicinal Herbs and Organic Crops in India*, CMA Monograph No. 224. Ahmedabad: CMA, IIM.

Chamber, A. 2015. 'Building Enabling Environment for Contract Farming Success', USAID Policy Brief No. 6, February. USAID.

Chazovachii, B., C. Mawere, and L. Chitongo. 2021. 'Sustainability of centralised contract farming among tobacco smallholder farmers in Makoni north district, Zimbabwe'. *Cogent Social Sciences* 7: 1–14.

Dev, S. M., and N. C. Rao. 2005. 'Food Processing and Contract Farming in Andhra Pradesh – A Small Farmer Perspective'. *Economic and Political Weekly* 40(26): 2705–2713.

FAO. 2012. *Guiding principles for responsible contract farming operations*. Rome: FAO.

FAO and IISD. 2018. *Model Agreement for Responsible Contract Farming, With Commentary*. Rome: FAO.

Glover, D. 1987. 'Increasing the Benefits to Smallholders from Contract Farming: Problems for Farmers' Organisations and Policy Makers'. *World Development* 15(4): 441–448.

GoI (Govt. of India). 2003. *Contract Farming Agreement and its Model Specifications*, 17 September. New Delhi: Ministry of Agriculture, Department of Agriculture and Co-operation, Krishi Bhawan.

ILSR (Institute for Local Self-Reliance). n.d. 'Protecting Contract Growers—Iowa Producer Protection Act'. Available at https://ilsr.org/rule/protecting-contract-growers/2062-2/ (accessed July 2023).

Lambrecht, I. B., and C. Ragasa. 2018. 'Do Development Projects Crowd-Out Private Sector Activities? Evidence from Contract Farming Participation in Northern Ghana'. *Food Policy* 74: 9–22.

MoAFW. 2017. *Model Act [The State/UT Agricultural Produce and Livestock Marketing (Promotion and Facilitation) Act, 2017]*, April. MoAFW, Department of Agriculture, Co-operation and Farmers' Welfare, Government of India.

MoAFW. 2020. *The Farmers Produce Trade and Commerce (Promotion and Facilitation) Bill*, No. 10 of 2020, Ministry of Agriculture and Farmer Welfare (MoAFW), Government of India.

Morris, S. 2007. 'Agriculture: A Perspective from History, the Metrics of Comparative Advantage and Limitations of the Market to Understand the Role of State in Globalising World', WP No. 2007-02-02, February. Ahmedabad: IIM.

Pande, S. 2008. 'Firm on the farm'. *Business Today* 19(16), 8 August: 46–48.

Pultrone, C. 2012. 'An Overview of Contract Farming: Legal Issues and Challenges'. *Uniform Law Review* 17: 263–289.

Purohit, P., K. S. Imai, and K. Sen. 2017. 'Do Agricultural Marketing Laws Matter for Rural Growth? Evidence from the Indian States', Discussion paper series DP2017-17, RIEB. Kobe, Japan: Kobe University.

Rickson, Roy E., and David Burch. 1996. 'Contract farming in organisational agriculture: The effects upon farmers and the environment'. In D. Burch, R. E. Rickson, and G. Lawrence (eds), *Globalisation and Agri-Food Restructuring—Perspectives from the Australasia Region,* 173–20. Brookfield (USA): Avebury.

Sako, M. 1992. *Prices, Quality and Trust—Inter-firm Relations in Britain and Japan.* Cambridge: CUP.

Shah, M. 2021. 'Reading K N Raj in the Age of Free Market Fundamentalism'. *Economic and Political Weekly* 56(14): 33–38.

Shrimali, R. 2014. 'Spaces of corporate control in agriculture: A critical study of contract farming in the Indian state of Punjab', PhD thesis. Toronto: York University.

Singh, G., and S. R. Asokan. 2005. *Contract Farming in India—Text and Cases.* New Delhi: Oxford & IBH.

Singh, J. 2003. 'Contracted green peas dumped in open market', 28 March, *The Tribune*, Chandigarh, p. 15.

Singh, M. P. 2007. 'Contract Farming and Emerging Agrarian Structure: The Case of Punjab', PhD thesis. New Delhi: CSRD, JNU.

Singh, R. 2008. 'Effectiveness of Contract Farming Practices for Agricultural Development and Equity: A Case of Hoshiarpur District in Punjab', Unpublished report. New Delhi: Oxfam International.

Singh, S. 2000a. 'Theory and Practice of Contract Farming—A Review'. *Journal of Social and Economic Development* 2(2), July–December: 228–246.

Singh, S. 2000b. 'Contract Farming for Agricultural Diversification in the Indian Punjab: A Study of Performance and Problems'. *Indian Journal of Agricultural Economics* 56(3), July–September: 283–294.

———. 2000c. 'Co-operative as Contractor: A case study of contract farming by a co-operative marketing federation in the Indian Punjab'. *Co-operative Perspective* 35(2).

———. 2001. 'Multi-National Corporations and Agricultural Technology Transfer: A Case Study of Contract Farming in the Indian Punjab'. In P. Chandra Shekara (ed.), *Private Extension: Indian Experiences*, 33–45. Hyderabad: MANAGE.

———. 2002a. 'Contracting Out Solutions: Political Economy of Contract Farming in the Indian Punjab'. *World Development* 30(9): 1621–38.

———. 2002b. 'Contract Farming: Let Firms, Farmers Deal Directly', 23 December, *The Tribune*, Chandigarh, p. 13.

———. 2004. 'Crisis and Diversification in Punjab Agriculture—Role of State and Agribusiness'. *Economic and Political Weekly* 39(52), 25 December.

———. 2005a. 'Role of the State in Contract Farming in Thailand: Experience and Lessons'. *ASEAN Economic Bulletin* 22(2): 217–228 (now *Journal of Southeast Asian Economies* from 2013).

———. 2005b. 'Contract Farming System in Thailand'. *Economic and Political Weekly* 40(53), 31 December: 5578–5586.

———. 2007. 'Contract Farming for Agricultural Development in Gujarat: Evidence and Issues'. In R. H. Dholakia (ed.), *Frontiers of Agricultural Development in Gujarat*. Ahmedabad: IIM.

———. 2008a. 'Understanding Practice of Contract Farming in India—A Small Producer Perspective'. In A. Gulati, P. K. Joshi, and M. Landes (eds), *Contract Farming in India: A Resource Book*. ICAR, IFPRI and USDA.

———. 2008b. 'Marketing Channels and their Implications for Smallholder Farmers in India'. In E. B. McCullough, P. L. Pingali, and K. G. Stamoulis (eds), *The Transformation of Agri-food Systems: Globalization, Supply Chains, and Smallholder Farmers*. Rome: FAO and London: Earthscan Press, 279–310.

———. 2008c. 'Producer Companies as New Generation Co-operatives'. *Economic and Political Weekly* 34(20), 17 May: 22–24.

Singh, S. 2008d. 'Gender and Child Labour in Cottonseed Production in India: A Case Study of Gujarat'. *Indian Journal of Labour Economics* 51(3): 445–458.

_____. 2009a. 'Supply Chains for High Value Crops: A Case Study of Mint in Punjab'. *Indian Journal of Agricultural Marketing* 23(1): 93–102.

_____. 2009b. *Organic Produce Supply Chains in India: Organisation and Governance*. New Delhi: Allied Publishers.

_____. 2011. 'Contract Farming for Sustainable Agricultural Development in India: A Smallholder Perspective', IGIDR Proceedings of Workshop on 'Policy Options and Investment Priorities for Accelerating Agricultural Productivity and Development in India' held at IIC, 10–11 November. New Delhi.

_____. 2012. *Modern Food Value Chains in India: Emerging Potential for the Poor*. New Delhi: Samskriti.

_____. 2013a. 'The Practice of Contract Farming in India: Making it Inclusive and Effective'. *Food Chain* 3(3): 137–154.

_____. 2013b. 'Regulating contract farming—Punjab way', 8 July, *The Tribune*, Chandigarh.

_____. 2015. 'Reforming markets, lessons from Bihar', 6 February, *The Tribune*, Chandigarh, Op. Ed. Agriculture, p. 9.

_____. 2016a. 'Smallholder Organisation through Farmer (Producer) Companies for Modern Markets: Experiences of Sri Lanka and India'. In Jos Bijman, Roldan Muradian, and Jur Schuurman (eds), *Cooperatives, Economic Democratization and Rural Development*, pp. 75–100. Edward Elgar Publishing.

_____. 2016b. 'Inclusive Food Value Chains in India: Evidence and Drivers'. In C. Ramasamy and K. R. Ashok (eds), *Vicissitudes of Indian Agriculture in a Growing Economy: Challenges, Strategies and the Way Forward*. New Delhi: Academic Foundation, and Mumbai: Indian Society of Agricultural Economics.

_____. 2021. *Understanding Performance and Impact of Producer Companies: Case Studies across States and Promoters in India*, Final report, March. Ahmedabad: CMA, IIM.

Singh, S., and T. Singh. 2014. *Producer Companies in India: Organisation and Performance*. New Delhi: Allied Publishers.

Vaswani, L. K., V. Venkatakrishnan, R. Upadhay, and J. Talati. 2003. *Agriculture-Market Linkages: Evaluating and Evolving a Conceptual Framework in Indian Context*, NABARD Occasional Paper No. 28. Mumbai: NABARD.

Wolf, S., B. Hueth, and E. Ligon. 2001. 'Policing Mechanisms in Agricultural Contracts'. *Rural Sociology* 66(3): 359–381.